PERELANDRA

GARDEN
WORKBOOK

II

Co-Creative Energy Processes
for Gardening, Agriculture
and Life

PERELANDRA

GARDEN

WORKBOOK

II

*Co-Creative Energy Processes
for Gardening, Agriculture
and Life*

MACHAELLE SMALL WRIGHT

PERELANDRA, LTD.

CENTER FOR NATURE RESEARCH
JEFFERSONTON ∕ VIRGINIA

This book is manufactured in the United States of America.
Designed by Machaelle Small Wright and James F. Brisson.
Cover design by James F. Brisson, Williamsville, VT 05362
Editing by the *Workbook II* Coning, David and Machaelle Small Wright.
Mechanical editing by Albert Schatz, Ph.D.
Copyediting by Beverly Beane.
Legwork, computer tech lifesaver, & meals by Clarence N. Wright.
Formatting, typesetting and computer wizardry
by Machaelle Small Wright.

This book was formatted, laid out and produced on an
AST Premium 286 computer using
the Xerox Ventura Publisher software along with
the Canon LBP-4 printer with an Eicon Laser Printer Adapter.

Printed on paper with recycled content.

Published by Perelandra, Ltd.,
P.O. Box 3603, Warrenton, VA 20188

Library of Congress Card Catalog Number: 87-90410
Wright, Machaelle Small
PERELANDRA GARDEN WORKBOOK II:
Co-Creative Energy Processes for
Gardening, Agriculture and Life

ISBN 0-927978-13-X

4 6 8 9 7 5

Table of Contents

Foreword

*The Old Order Changeth, Yielding Place to New**

by Albert Schatz, Ph.D.

Albert Einstein warned us that, "We shall require a substantially new manner of thinking if mankind is to survive." Machaelle Small Wright tells us that that "new . . . thinking" necessitates our understanding what a co-creative partnership with nature is. Her work also makes it crystal clear why our establishing a co-creative partnership with nature is our only hope for survival. Her *Workbook II* and other Perelandra publications are therefore quintessentially concerned with what is literally a matter of life or death.

My comments about Machaelle refer to both her and nature; that is, the nature intelligences that work with her in the co-creative partnership which she and nature have jointly established. My comments about Machaelle's work refer to the nature research which she does in collaboration with nature. Machaelle calls that research "co-creative science." Perelandra is their Nature Research Center, hers and nature's. The Perelandra garden is their laboratory. The Perelandra research staff consists of Machaelle and various intelligences. The nature intelligences include devas and overlighting devas, Pan and other nature spirits. The research staff also

* Alfred, Lord Tennyson

Dr. Schatz discovered the antibiotic Streptomycin, which was the first effective means of treating human tuberculosis. For this and other research, he received honorary degrees and medals, and was named an honorary member of scientific, medical and dental societies in Europe, Latin America and the U.S.

For these definitions, see the Introduction.

includes the White Brotherhood, Universal Light, and a host of other consciousnesses from different dimensions, levels, and bands of reality. To avoid ambiguity, Machaelle has provided us in *Workbook II* with definitions and other information about nature, nature intelligences, reality, consciousness, co-creative science, etc.

Man is now an endangered species. The global devastation of nature, which has already caused the extinction of many animal species, is now making this planet uninhabitable for man. That widespread devastation, which is increasing at an exponential rate, is caused by multinational corporations and what President Dwight Eisenhower called the military-industrial complex. These agencies use science to manipulate nature for profit in ways that violate the *World Charter for Nature*. That Charter, adopted by the General Assembly of the United Nations on October 28, 1982, states: "Every form of life is unique, warrenting respect regardless of its worth to man; and, to accord other organisms such recognition, man must be guided by a moral code of action . . . "

The Piscean era, from which we are moving, explored and worked with the dynamics of the parent/child, higher/lower and masculine-energy-dominant relationships; and expressed these dynamics in both action and structure throughout all levels of form reality.

The problem we face cannot be resolved by using contemporary science in ways that are less destructive to nature. The world has changed fundamentally and irreversibly; and now requires a different kind of science. The Overlighting Deva of Planet Earth explains the change that has occurred (chapter 12). Contemporary science was developed in the Piscean era during which man has had a parent/child relationship with nature. What we now need is the Aquarian dynamic of teamwork which co-creative science offers. The "new . . . thinking" that we need to survive includes our understanding and applying co-creative science. This science requires a co-creative partnership between man and nature. The "V" diagram on the following page represents graphically the origins of co-creative science and contemporary science, and their positions in man's evolutionary movement.

The Aquarian era into which we are moving emphasizes the concepts of balance, teamwork and partnership. These dynamics will be emphasized in the pattern and rhythm of life behavior.

Co-creative science is qualitatively different from contemporary science because it integrates the involutionary input of nature (order, organization, and life vitality) with the evolutionary dynamic (direction and purpose) of man. (These and other terms are defined in Machaelle's publications.) For man to obtain the involutionary

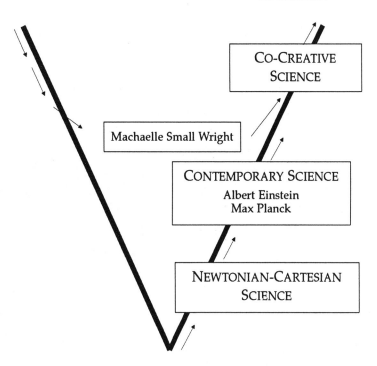

Newtonian-Cartesian Science, also known as Classical Science, developed in the 17th century. That science was based on the work of the physicist Sir Isaac Newton and the philosopher René Descartes. Contemporary, present-day science is based on the research of Max Planck, "the father of quantum mechanics" (1900), and Albert Einstein's theories of relativity (1905 and 1916).

input of nature, he must consciously establish a co-creative partnership with nature.

This partnership is qualitatively different from the one-sided relationship of people who, as they say, "work with nature." Those individuals, with the best of intentions, do what they rightly or wrongly assume nature wants. They unilaterally make decisions for themselves and for nature. Nature is not consulted. They do what they think is best for nature, just as one does what one thinks is best for a child. They treat nature like a child for whom "mother knows best."

In a co-creative partnership with nature, man quickly realizes that, where nature and involutionary matters are involved, nature knows best. Furthermore, man recognizes nature as extraordinarily knowledgeable and incredibly competent scientifically. One literally communicates with nature, discusses issues with nature, welcomes nature's input, and makes decisions jointly with nature—all the while exercising free will intelligently. This is how Machaelle functions in her Nature Research Center at Perelandra. Many people who have their own co-creative partnerships with nature also communicate (kinesiologically) with nature.

The balance of the involutionary dynamic of nature with the evolutionary dynamic of man is what distinguishes co-creative science. Contemporary science, on the other hand, results essentially from the evolutionary endeavors of man carried out independently of any input requested from nature within the framework of a co-creative partnership. Co-creative science is therefore not a linear advance over contemporary science. It is, instead, a qualitatively unique and hitherto unknown kind of science developed *de novo* by Machaelle and nature in their co-creative partnership. Co-creative science employs different methodologies than contemporary science does, and obtains information from intelligences with which contemporary scientists have never worked and whose existence would be derogated and denied.

YOU, TOO, CAN DO IT

Finally, there is something else about co-creative science that is particularly relevant to you. From the point of view of contemporary science, some people (depending on their training and what they do) are considered to be scientists; others are not. That distinction is usually quite clear. But from the point of view of nature, everybody can be a co-creative scientist. It is not difficult, expensive, or time-consuming.

You don't need formal training in science. You don't have to invest large amounts of money (registration fees, tuition fees, laboratory fees, etc.) and years working for an academic degree in science. You don't need any degree at all. You don't need a scientific laboratory or its equipment. Your garden, farm, classroom, business, home and hobby are suitable laboratories for co-creative science. The credentials you need are intent, sincerity, and commitment. You also need the processes, definitions, the kinesiological technique and other information available in Perelandra publications. You then start by establishing a co-creative partnership with nature, which you can do anywhere.

Co-creative science is much more than something to read about, think about, and find interesting. It is an applied science which has the most profound implications for all of us. If you do establish a co-creative partnership with nature and become involved in co-creative science, what you do may well be more important than what many so-called scientists are doing. This is one of many opportunities that the *Perelandra Garden Workbooks I and II* offer you.

DEFINITIONS

The intelligences with which Machaelle works can explain co-creative science much more adequately than I can. I therefore feel privileged to have Machaelle's and their permission to include the following definitions of science, nature, co-creative science, and philosophy which they communicated to Machaelle in a session. These definitions and the comments by Hyperithon (head of the Department of Science and Technology in the White Brotherhood) have not yet been published elsewhere (with the exception of the definition of nature).

❊ SCIENCE: *Science is the study of reality and how it works. It is an umbrella term in that it covers a large number of life schools, with each school focusing on a specific area of study. Science is also a term that expands in what it encompasses as an individual's or society's concept of reality expands. Consequently, science is prevalent on all levels of reality; yet what it enfolds is relative to a specific level at any given time. There is no one description of science beyond the study of reality and how it works that would apply to science as it is practiced on all levels and dimensions of life.*

However, we will say this: As the lines of communication open between scientific societies on one dimension or level and scientific societies on another dimension or level, you will see an interweaving of the information regarding reality and how it works on each level. This interwoven information will automatically create a larger picture of the whole. What we are saying is that individuals working in related areas of science but on different levels, and therefore independently of one another, will eventually link, and an immediate sharing of the information will result.

This linking cannot be forced. Nor can it be initiated by devices, instruments or machines. It will occur within the heart, mind and soul of each scientist and will be triggered by intent. In this way, as a general rule, the linking will remain intimately connected with the timing of the scientist and the society in which he works.

In another session, Hyperithon informed Machaelle that,

> science is the study of reality and how reality functions . . . When one is referring to reality in form, one must include nature. This is because all form is nature. On the form levels, spirit and nature's matter come together in the most intimate of partnerships. Consequently, it is not only appropriate but essential that science, within any level of form, be studied through the arena of nature. To try to understand reality and how it works outside the arena of nature is to totally miss the point.

❁ NATURE: . . . *Nature is a massive, intelligent consciousness group that expresses and functions within the many areas of involution, that is, moving soul-oriented consciousness into any dimension or level of form.*

The complete definition of nature is on page 4.

Nature is the conscious reality that supplies order, organization and life vitality for this shift. Nature is the consciousness that is, for your working understanding, intimately linked with form. Nature is the consciousness that comprises all form on all levels and dimensions. It is form's order, organization and life vitality. Nature is first and foremost a consciousness of equal importance with all other consciousnesses in the largest scheme of reality. It expresses and functions uniquely in that it comprises all form on all levels and dimensions and is responsible for and creates all of form's order, organization and life vitality.

❁ CO-CREATIVE SCIENCE: *The scientific research at Perelandra is an example of co-creative science because it involves the linking of science on two levels, each with its own specific understanding of reality. On the one hand, we have reality as understood and practiced by the human soul; on the other hand, we have reality as understood and practiced by nature. This particular linking is especially vital because all life, as expressed in form, is the coming together of these two levels.*

For reality in form to function in balance and with a full and wide range of options, there must be not only the coming together of soul and matter, but also understanding of the soul dynamic and how it works, and the nature dynamic and how that works. In addition, there must be understanding of the combined soul/nature dynamic and how it works as a unit. Up to the present time, the scientific community on the Earth level has separated the study of soul dynamics from nature dynamics. It has created two separate schools: the evolutionary, human-dominant school in which the human potential is studied; and the evolutionary, nature-dominant school that studies the natural sciences.

To understand reality and how it works within form on the Earth level, the two schools must be linked. But the necessary link cannot be found in the two schools as they are presently set up. That link lies in the unit of the soul dynamic and the nature dynamic as expressed in all form. If one is to understand reality and how it works on the Earth level, one must focus on the reality as demonstrated in the soul/form unit. The key to the next major scientific study is in this focus. The foundation for all future scientific expansions that will occur between levels and dimensions lies in this focus. It is both the key to future discoveries and the foundation of those discoveries.

❀ PHILOSOPHY: *From our perspective, philosophy is the scientific study of organized human thought, ideas and perceptions, their patterns and how they link together to play an historic role as one dynamic of the human evolutionary movement. It is also a scientific "lab" through which organized human thought, ideas and perceptions may be introduced to society. As a science, it catalogs and defines what is already reflected in society during specific historic periods and it serves in a leadership capacity to introduce "the next step" into that society.*

*We might add here that all schools of science, if they are to operate from a position of balance, must research what is already part of society, **and** they must also serve as portals through which the next step can be introduced to that society. If only research of what is already integrated in* *society is done, this particular scientific area will stall and begin to stagnate. If only the new is sought, there will be no sense of a building-block foundation. Also, timing, patterning and how the new fits into the larger picture will be missed. Contributions will therefore appear to be "alien." The society will most likely reject such new information which comes out of an unbalanced school.*

OUR SACRED COVENANT WITH NATURE

What follows is, in nature's own words, the responsibility that nature has for man. These comments, which nature communicated to Machaelle for the book, *Flower Essences*, will enable you to more clearly understand that we have betrayed our partnership, contractual agreement, and sacred covenant with nature; that, in so doing, we have also betrayed ourselves; and why collaboration with nature (and nature has told us how to collaborate) is now our only hope for survival.

Overlighting Deva Of Flower Essences

I am part of what might be called "the healing devas," in that I am a part of a group of overlighting intelligences in nature who focus specifically on the various healing dynamics within and throughout the kingdoms of nature on planet Earth.

When the human soul chose to inspirit physical matter on the planet, we of nature consciously accepted a partnership with humans that related to the development of their physical form and all matters relating to what may best be described as the upkeep and maintenance of that form in every way. In present-day terminology, you may say that we have a "contractual agreement" with you humans which was initiated prior to the human soul coming to the planet and was fully activated the very instant the first souls entered the planet's atmosphere. Nature has been completely at your disposal as you took on matter and developed your form. All that comprises human form is extracted from the three kingdoms of nature.

But form development and its maintenance through food, shelter and clothing is only a part of our agreement. In light of the universal law of horizontal healing, we also took on the responsibility to balance the human form during times of dysfunction. So in these areas we have overlighting healing devas who establish the patterns in nature that respond to human form in healing ways and integrate those patterns into the specific blueprint of individual plants, animals and minerals to be recognized, unlocked and used appropriately by humans when needed.

The following comments are taken from Perelandra Paper #4, *Body/Soul Fusion Process: A Flower Essence Process for Newborns, Infants, Older Children and Adults.*

The fusion of the body and soul can be seen as symbolic of the sacred contract that exists between humans and nature. In order for the human soul to experience life within the band of form, it is essential that the soul combine with form and function as a working unit. Nature is the dynamic in reality that creates, orders, organizes and adds life vitality to all of form. It is from the nature dynamic itself that form is created. For a human soul to function within the band of form, it must unite with nature—in essence, form a partnership with nature. This partnership is at the very core of the sacred contract that nature has accepted with human souls as well as with spirits from all dimensions of reality that wish to experience life within the band of form. Nature has agreed to work together with soul dynamics in order to create and establish functioning body/soul units. The soul initiates and inspirits the partnership, and nature supplies the appropriate combination of form elements through which the soul functions. The soul initiates and nature responds accordingly.

FROM ONE SCIENTIST TO ANOTHER

Sit down before fact like a little child, and be prepared to give up every preconceived notion, follow humbly wherever and to whatever abyss nature leads, or you shall learn nothing. —T. H. HUXLEY

I began with Einstein and will end with Machaelle. Both have given us new understandings of reality, nature, and the world. But here the similarity ends. Einstein's relativity theories (along with Planck's quantum mechanics, Bell's theorem, Bohm's implicate and explicate orders, the many worlds theory, and *all* other aspects of contemporary science based on the new physics) are limited, but not by language. They are limited by the parameters of man's evolutionary knowledge and ability within which they were developed. They lack the involutionary input of nature which Machaelle's co-creative science includes.

Werner Heinsenberg recognized that limitation when he wrote, "What we observe is not nature itself, but nature exposed to our method of questioning." Wolfgang Pauli also recognized that limitation when he created his "irrationality of reality." Co-creative science has no uncertainty principle and no irrationality of reality.

The limitations of contemporary science have been definitively surveyed and mapped by Kurt Gödel. According to Larry Dossey (in *Recovering the Soul*) Gödel's incompleteness theorems "have been scrutinized by mathematicians and logicians of the highest caliber for over half a century and have not been shown to contain inconsistencies." Gödel's incompleteness theorems

> . . . strike at the heart of science's ideal aim, which is to devise a complete and consistent picture of nature. Gödel showed that this cannot be done. Not only is it not technically possible to accumulate all the data necessary to formulate such a picture, the very goal itself is hopeless. Gödel's theorems show that nature's laws, if they *are* consistent, as we believe them to be, must be of some inner formulation quite different from anything we now know, as Jacob Bronowski put it, and which at present "we have no idea how to conceive."

It is not surprising that Gödel's theorems are largely ignored by the scientific community. Life is much simpler if "reality *is* in the eyes of the beholder." And that is precisely what the new physics postulates; namely, that we, with our intent and our consciousness, create reality, nature, ourselves, and everything else in the universe. According to Henry Margenau, "The physicist does not discover, he creates his universe." And C. W. Williams believes that, "A new world is only a new mind."

Gary Zukav (in *The Dancing Wu Li Masters*) describes how this man-made version of reality was manufactured.

Reality is what we take to be true. What we take to be true is what we believe. What we believe is based upon our perceptions. What we perceive depends upon what we look for. What we look for depends on what we think. What we think depends on what we perceive. What we perceive determines what we believe. What we believe determines what we take to be true. What we take to be true is our reality.

Dossey (in *Space, Time & Medicine*) comments on this as follows.

It is a common, almost uniform mistake to assume that science can resolve for us what is meant by "real." It is unsettling to discover that modern physical scientists no longer make any claim to reality, seeking instead to give only the best description of the world they can devise, and one that rests entirely on sense impressions. The quest for reality is an antiquated one in modern science, belonging to an era that ended with the advent of this century.

Scientists who are interested in reality should read *Universal Light Describes Itself* and other Perelandra publications which quote the intelligences with whom Machaelle works. *Verbum satis sapienti.*

They are also well-advised to seriously consider the following comments by Hyperithon.

Dr. Schatz assures me that this means, "A word to the wise is sufficient." We all knew that, didn't we!

> *. . . there are fundamental "holes" existing in the science known as "quantum physics." Quantum physics as a scientific framework was an essential step in expanding the human consciousness to encompass a greater understanding of how "things" work. The holes could not and cannot be resolved within the framework of quantum physics itself. But until recently, the holes, as you call them, did not create a stumbling block regarding the expansion process that quantum physics has triggered within the human consciousness.*
>
> *Interestingly enough, what has brought the issues of the quantum physics holes to the forefront has been the massive pressure placed on humankind from the direction of ecology. The world situation is such at the present time that the solutions to*

the pressing ecological problems cannot come exclusively from the framework of quantum physics. The holes, once demonstrated in action and form within nature and regarding ecology, will only be emphasized that much more. Quantum physics functions as a bridge step in science . . . It was not designed to remain "in force" over a long period of time.

For Machaelle, reality is in the eyes of nature and the other intelligences with whom she communicates and does research. Co-creative science is qualitatively different from all other sciences because it includes the involutionary input of nature and other intelligences whose knowledge and ability are beyond our comprehension. Those intelligences are another important source of information with which humans can communicate. Einstein believed that " . . . all knowledge about reality begins with experience and terminates with it." But Einstein's experience was the ordinary experience with which we are all familiar. Machaelle's experience, with nature and other intelligences, is far beyond that.

Henry P. Stapp considers Bell's theory to be the most important contribution in the history of science. But Stapp does not know about co-creative science. I am convinced that Machaelle's research with nature and co-creative science are the most important advance in the history of science.

Preface

As I was writing this book, I kept getting an overwhelming urge to turn to you, the reader, and say "Relax! Take it easy. Don't get in a sweat about all this." So, I'm using this preface to say just that to you. For some of you who have been using the first *Perelandra Garden Workbook*, this second book will make all kinds of sense. For others who have worked with the first *Workbook*, the processes presented in *Workbook II* may hit you a bit between the eyes. That's because this is the next step, and next steps have the tendency to catch us off guard. When that happens, just take a deep breath, remind yourself to relax—and keep reading.

One thing that might help you take this next step is to know that all the processes presented in *Workbook II* have gone through "test trials." This is much of what nature and I do at Perelandra. We explore and then create co-creative processes that facilitate that next step. For the past two and a half years, we have been working on the *Workbook II* processes. And we have tried them out in the Perelandra garden. During that time, I have given some of the processes to others to try out. They work just as well for others as they do for me.

This leads to the next point. I realize that some of you feel that *I* can do these processes with nature because I have "special gifts." First of all, I don't have any more in the "special-gift department" than anyone else who has a natural leaning and has applied himself mightily to discipline, hone and develop that natural leaning into a craft, art or profession.

We, nature and I, work hard to develop processes that can easily be applied by *anyone* who is interested in developing a co-creative relationship with nature. These processes are not meant for the mythical "special few." We're not interested in creating a cult. Our efforts are directed to assisting growth and change within the state of nature on this planet and in how people relate to nature. By definition, since nature isn't exclusively available to a special few, this includes everyone. All you have to do is *want* to work with nature in a co-creative partnership.

I sometimes run into another misconception about working with the co-creative processes that come out of Perelandra. Some believe that the processes work only if the person doing the process can feel it working in some special and unique way. Besides being baloney, this attitude gives those folks who experience life through the five senses, as we know them, the feeling that they are not capable of developing a co-creative relationship with nature because they aren't "sensitive" enough. Please, people—I can't adequately express how much hogwash this is. If someone tries to impress upon you that *he* uses the Perelandra processes and that *he* knows that co-creative work with nature requires special sensitivity, just ignore him. He's expressing his need to feel special or important.

The truth is, you don't have to feel anything above and beyond what your usual five senses tell you in order to do the Perelandra processes and for these processes to work. They are developed so that all you need to do is move through each one, step by step, doing precisely what is spelled out. Nature automatically and appropriately joins in as you move through the steps. You will be doing your part of the process and nature will be doing its part of the process. You may move through an entire series of processes feeling absolutely nothing of what nature has been doing or of the changes the processes have initiated. However, I guarantee you that after completing the processes you will notice a difference that you will not be able to explain away with conventional reasoning or

excuses. You will see changes in patterns and refinements in form—
and then you will know that the processes worked.

One other thing may happen. You and nature have worked
together with the processes. You didn't feel a thing, but you have a
gut feeling that everything went as it should. You're going along
with the rest of your day as usual and, all of a sudden, something
catches your eye. A brilliant flower blooming where you *know* a
flower wasn't growing the day before. An unusual and dramatic
aerial show being put on by birds who don't normally do this kind
of thing. A strong flower scent, like a spring bouquet, where there
are no flowers. A cloud formation that is so unusual that it stops
you in your tracks. Don't brush those moments off. This is nature
saying "Thank you." They are connecting with you through your
five senses by doing something that is just enough out of the ordinary to catch your attention. Just smile and say "You're welcome."

Now, there might be some confusion about my use of the word
"Workbook" throughout this book. After all, there are now two
workbooks—*Perelandra Garden Workbook* and *Perelandra Garden
Workbook: Part II.* When I use "Workbook," I am referring to the first
book, *Perelandra Garden Workbook.* When I refer to the book you are
now reading, I use "*Workbook II.*"

There is one other potential point of confusion: You will note that
the subtitle of the *Workbook* is *A Complete Guide to Gardening with
Nature Intelligences.* It begs the question: If it is complete, why is
there a *Workbook II?*

At the time that I wrote the Workbook, I thought it was complete.
Well, I found out it was only complete unto itself. Now we have
Workbook II, an expansion of the first *Workbook.* I will not be so silly
as to again suggest that the co-creative partnership is now defined
and complete with the publication of *Workbook II.* I suspect there
will be a *Workbook III.*

PERELANDRA

GARDEN
WORKBOOK

II

Co-Creative Energy Processes
for Gardening, Agriculture
and Life

*To the
continuing growth
and development in this
extraordinary partnership
we humans have with
nature.*

Introduction

Back in November, 1989, Albert Schatz, Ph.D., ordered the *Workbook*. With his order, he sent a letter to me letting me know that his background was in soil science—soil chemistry and soil microbiology, to be exact. He is a professor emeritus at Temple University, and he was planning to write a book called *The Living Soil* and wanted to include information about nature or elemental spirits.

Well, he intrigued me. So I fired off a copy of the *Workbook* and waited to see if I'd ever hear from him again. A week later, I got another letter. He had spent the week "studying" the *Workbook*, and wrote this:

> . . . The book I plan to write will not only compare the soil to a living organism, but actually define it as such. I have been planning to write this book for several years, but I did not do so because I felt "something was missing," and I did not know what it was. When I read the *Workbook*, I knew; or, I should say, I recognized what I had been sensing as "something missing". . . . You have given me precisely the information I need to write the book I have been thinking of for several years . . .

Since this letter, Dr. Schatz and I have stayed in close contact. He has read, studied (he makes a distinction between reading and

In case you didn't read the Preface, let me again clarify that when I use the word "Workbook," I am referring to the first book, Perelandra Garden Workbook. *When I refer to the book you are now reading, I use "Workbook II."*

studying!) and worked with the Perelandra material. He has been invaluable to me in a number of ways, and one way is that he has shown me how the Perelandra work as a co-creative science fits into the larger scientific picture. He has tapped into his scientific knowledge to verify for me that nature *really* does know what it is talking about. For example, in the *Workbook* we have the Soil Balancing Process that works with the soil to a depth of five feet. I never understood why nature wanted this process to cover a five-foot depth. To be honest, it didn't matter to me that much. Nature said to do it, so that's what I did. In Dr. Schatz's second letter, he commented about the Soil Balancing Process.

> . . . The other point I want to make is about the necessity, in the Soil Balancing Process, to consider the soil to a depth of five feet. That makes sense because the soil, as a living organism, has a physical body. That physical body may be two, three, four or even five feet deep, if one also includes what is called the "parent material" of the soil itself. And many plant roots go down that far.
>
> If one works with only the top layer (6-12") of the soil, one is not working with the soil as a *whole* organism . . .

So the mystery of the five feet was cleared up.

As Dr. Schatz studied the Perelandra material, he began to express the need for me to "sit down with nature" and get them to define some terms that are frequently used in the nature sessions and work at Perelandra. He suspected that nature's definitions of these words were not the same as the traditional definitions. He felt that without these definitions, we weren't going to be able to fully grasp what nature is saying to us and teaching us. And like any person with a fifty-year background in science and education, Dr. Schatz gave me a "suggested" list that he felt needed definitions from nature!

Well, Dr. Schatz was right. Nature's definitions are not exactly what you and I normally assume when we use words like form, nature, energy, reality, consciousness, soul . . . And he was right about nature's definitions giving us a much deeper insight into what is happening at Perelandra and into the whole co-creative partnership that is developing between nature and us. They are both profound and eye-opening.

I include these definitions in this book right up front because I feel they will help you understand why the energy processes were developed, why they work and why it is imperative that we include these energy processes in our work with nature. We need them, nature needs them and, quite frankly, the planet needs them.

CO-CREATIVE DEFINITIONS DEALING WITH NATURE, LIFE, SCIENCE, THE UNIVERSE AND ALL ELSE

Let us give you the basic understanding of these terms. We feel that these definitions, kept short and simple, will be more helpful than lengthy, detailed ones. Consider these definitions to be starting points.

❋ **FORM:** *We consider reality to be in the form state when there is organization, order and life vitality combined with a state of consciousness. For the purpose of understanding form in a constructive and workable manner, let us say that we consider consciousness to be soul-initiated and, therefore, quite capable of function beyond what we would term "form." There are dimensions of reality in which the interaction of life reality is maintained on the level of consciousness only. There is no surrounding organization, order or life vitality as we know it. There is only consciousness.*

We do not consider form to be only that which is perceptible to the five senses. In fact, we see form from this perspective to be most limited, both in its life reality and in its ability to function. We see form from the perspective of the five senses to be useful only for the most basic and fundamental level of identification. From this perspective, there is very little relationship to the full understanding and knowledge of how a unit or form system functions.

*All energy contains order, organization and life vitality; therefore, **all energy is form.** If one were to use the term "form" to identify that which can be perceived by the basic senses and the word "energy" to refer to that aspect of an animal, human, plant or object's reality that cannot be readily perceived by the basic senses, then one would be accurate in the use of* *these two words. However, if one were to use the word "form" to refer to that which can be perceived by the basic five senses and assume form to be a complete unit of reality unto itself, and use the word "energy" to refer to a level beyond form, one would then be using these two words inaccurately.*

On the planet Earth, the personality, character, emotional makeup, intellectual capacity, strong points and gifts of a human are all form. They are that which gives order, organization and life vitality to consciousness.

Order and organization are the physical structures that create a framework for form. In short, they define the walls. But we have included the dynamic of life vitality when we refer to form because one of the elements of form is action, and it is the life vitality that initiates and creates action.

❈ **NATURE:** *In the larger universe and beyond, on its many levels and dimensions, there are a number of groups of consciousnesses which, although equal in importance, are quite different in expression and function. Do not misunderstand us by thinking that we are saying that all reality is human soul-oriented but that there are some aspects of this reality that function and express differently. We are not saying this. We are saying that there are different groups of consciousnesses that are equal in importance but express and function very differently. Together, they comprise the full expression of the larger, total life picture. No one piece, no one expression, can be missing or the larger life picture on all its levels and dimensions will cease to exist. One such consciousness has been universally termed "nature." Because of what we are saying about the larger picture not existing without all of its parts, you may assume that nature as both a reality and a consciousness exists on all dimensions and all levels. It cannot be excluded.*

Each group of consciousnesses has what can be termed as an area of expertise. As we said, all groups are equal in importance but express and function differently from one another. These different expressions and functions are vital to the overall balance of reality. A truly symbiotic relationship exists among the groups and is based on balance—universal balance. You are absolutely correct to characterize the human soul-oriented dynamic as evolution in scope and function. And you are correct in identifying the nature dynamic as being involution in scope and function. Nature is a massive, intelligent consciousness group that expresses and functions within the many areas of involution, that is, moving soul-oriented consciousness into any dimension or level of form.

Nature is the conscious reality that supplies order, organization and life vitality for this shift. Nature is the consciousness that is, for your working understanding, intimately linked with form. Nature is the consciousness that comprises all form on all levels and dimensions. It is form's order, organization and life vitality. Nature is first and foremost a consciousness of equal importance with all other consciousnesses in the largest scheme of reality. It expresses and functions uniquely in that it comprises all form on all levels and dimensions and is responsible for and creates all of form's order, organization and life vitality.

❀ **DEVAS AND NATURE SPIRITS:** *"Devas" and "nature spirits" are names used to identify two different expressions and functions within the nature consciousness. They are the two groups within the larger nature consciousness that interface with the human soul while in form. There are other groups, and they are differentiated from one another primarily by specific expression and function.*

To expand from our definition of form, it is the devic expression that fuses with consciousness to create order, organization and life vitality. The devic expression as the architect designs the complex order, organization and life vitality that will be needed by the soul consciousness while functioning within the scope or band of form. If the consciousness chooses to shift from one point of form to another point, thereby changing form function, it is the devic expression of nature that alters the organization, order and life vitality accordingly. The devic expression designs and is the creation of the order, organization and life vitality of form.

The nature spirit expression infuses the devic order, organization and life vitality and adds to this the dynamic of function and working balance. To order, organization and life vitality it brings movement and the bond that maintains the alignment of the devic form unit to the universal principles of balance while the consciousness is in form.

To say that nature is the expert in areas of form and form principles barely scratches the surface of the true nature (pardon the pun) of nature's role in form. It is the expert of form and it is form itself. A soul-oriented consciousness cannot exist on any level or dimension of form in any way *without an **equal**, intimate, symbiotic relationship with the nature consciousness.*

❀ **CONSCIOUSNESS**: *The concept of consciousness has been vastly misunderstood. To put it simply, consciousness is the working state of the soul. In human expression, as one sees it demonstrated on the planet Earth, the personality, character, emotional makeup, intellectual capacity, strong points and gifts of a human are all form. They are that which gives order, organization and life vitality to consciousness.*

We say "working state of the soul" because there are levels of soul existence that are different than the working state and can best be described as a simple and complete state of being. The closest that souls on Earth come to this notion is the state of unconsciousness. But this is to give you a glimpse of what we mean by "state of being." We urge you not to assume that what you know as unconsciousness is equal to the soul state of being.

Humans tend to think of the soul as being something that exists far away from them because they are in form. This is an illusion. The core of any life is the soul. It cannot exist apart from itself. Like the heart in the human body, it is an essential part of the life unit. A human in form is, by definition, a soul fused with nature. Personality and character are a part of the nature/form package that allows the soul to function and to express itself in form. They are not the soul; they are the order and organization of that soul.

Consciousness physically fuses into the body system first through the electrical system and then through the central nervous system and the brain. This is another aspect of nature supplying order, organization and life vitality. Consciousness itself cannot be measured or monitored as a reality. But what can be measured and monitored is the order, organization and life vitality of consciousness. Consciousness is the working state of the soul and is not form. It is nature, not consciousness, that supplies form.

We wish to add a thought here so that there will be no confusion about the relationship between nature and the soul. The devic level of nature does not, with its own power, superimpose its interpretation of form onto a soul. We have said that nature and soul are intimately and symbiotically related. This implies a give and take. No one consciousness group operates in isolation of the whole or of all other parts of the whole. When a soul chooses to move within the vast band of form, it communicates its intent and purpose to nature. It is from this that nature, on the devic level, derives the specifics that will be needed for the soul to function in form. It is a perfect marriage of purpose with the order, organization and life vitality that is needed for the fulfillment of that purpose. Nature, therefore, does not define purpose and impose it on a soul. It orders, organizes and gives life vitality to purpose for expression of form.

✤ **SOUL:** *We perceive that most likely the question of soul will arise with anyone reading these definitions. This will be most difficult to define since the soul is, at its point of central essence, beyond form. Consequently, it is beyond words. However, it is not beyond any specific life form. As we have said, an individual is not separate or distant from his or her soul. Souls, as individuated life forces, were created in form at the moment you call the "Big Bang." Beyond form, souls are also beyond the notion of creation. So we refer to the moment of the Big Bang regarding the soul, since this gives you a description of soul that will be most meaningful to you.*

The Big Bang was the nature-designed order, organization and life force used to differentiate soul into sparks of individuated light energy. The power of the Big Bang was created by intent. And that intent originated from the massive collective soul reality beyond form.

It is reasonable to look at the Big Bang as the soul's gateway to the immense band of form. To perceive the soul and how it functions exclusively from the perspective of human form on Earth is akin to seeing that planet from the perspective of one grain of sand. The soul's options of function and expression in form are endless. What we see occurring more frequently now on Earth is the shift from the individual soul unknowingly functioning in an array of options, all chosen only because they are compatible to the immediate purpose of the soul, to the individual beginning to function with discrimination and intent in more expanded ways. Using the words in their more limited, parochial definitions, we can say that we see the beginning of a shift from soul function in which an individuated personality remains unaware of many of its options to soul function in which the personality begins to take on conscious awareness of all its options.

✤ **ENERGY:** *For those experiencing life on Earth, energy is form that is perceived by an individual beyond the scope of the basic five senses. All energy contains order, organization and life vitality; therefore, all energy is form. The makeup and design of the specific order, organization and life* vitality within that which can be perceived by the basic five senses is identical to and therefore harmonious with its broader reality, which cannot be perceived by the basic five senses. If one is to use the term "form" to identify that which can be perceived by the basic senses and the word "energy" to refer to that aspect of an animal, human, plant or object's reality that cannot be readily perceived by the basic senses, then one would be accurate in the use of these two words. However, if one is to use the word "form" to refer to that which can be perceived by the basic five senses and assume form to be a complete unit of reality unto itself, and use the word "energy" to refer to a level beyond form, one would then be using these two words inaccurately. From our perspective, form and energy create one unit of reality and are differentiated from one another solely by the individual's ability to perceive them with his or her sensory system. In short, the differentiation between that which is form and that which is energy within any given object, plant, animal or human lies with the observer.

❀ **BASIC SENSORY SYSTEM PERCEPTION:** We define basic sensory system perception as being that which the vast majority of individuals on Earth experience. The acts of seeing, hearing, touching, tasting and smelling fall within what we acknowledge as a basic, fundamental range of sensory development that is predominant on the Earth level. What is referred to as an "expansion experience" is, in fact, an act or experience that is perceived by an individual because of an expansion of the range in which his sensory system operates. Expansion experiences are not perceived outside or beyond an individual's electrical system, central nervous system and sensory system. These three systems are interrelated, and an accurate perception of an expansion experience requires that the three systems operate in concert. Therefore, it is quite possible for something to occur in an individual's life that registers in the person's electrical system and central nervous system but then short-circuits, is altered or is blocked simply because the person's present sensory system does not have the ability to process, due to its present range of operation, what has registered in the other two systems. People say that "these kinds of strange things never happen to me." This is inaccurate. "Strange" things, experiences and moments beyond the present state of their sensory systems, are continuously happening around them and to them. They are simply not at the point where their sensory systems are capable of clear, useful processing. They *waste time by directing their will and focus to "make things happen." That is useless since things are happening all the time around them. Instead they should relax and continue through an organic developmental process that is already in effect and which will gradually allow them to accurately perceive what is happening around them. In some cases, where events or experiences are vaguely perceived or processed in outrageous, useless ways, their sensory system is expanding but still not operating within the range where events can be usefully processed.*

❋ **REALITY:** *From our perspective, reality refers to all levels and dimensions of life experience within form and beyond form. Reality does not depend on an individual's perception of it in order to exist. We call an individual's perception of reality his "perceived reality." Any life system that was created in form (which occurred at the moment of the Big Bang) has inherent in it all dimensions and levels that exist both within form and beyond. How we relate to an individual or object depends on our present ability to enfold and envelop an individual's many levels. The scope within which one exists, the reality of one's existence, is truly beyond form, beyond description. If one understands that the evolutionary force which moves all life systems forward is endless—beyond time—then one must also consider that it is the continuous discovery of these vast levels inherent in all life systems that creates that evolutionary momentum. Since that dynamic is beyond time as expressed on any form level or dimension, it is endless.*

❋ **PERCEIVED REALITY:** *This is the combination of elements that make up an individual's full system of reality and are perceived, embraced and enfolded by him or by another individual at any given time. From this, an individual "knows" himself or another individual only from the perspective of the specific combination of elements he or she is able to perceive, embrace and enfold. Any one element can be considered a window to the larger whole. When in form, these elements take on the dynamics of order, organization and life vitality and are demonstrated through these specific form frameworks. The extent to which perceived reality corresponds to the larger, all-encompassing reality depends on the ability of an individual to accurately demonstrate these elements within form frameworks and the ability of that or another individual to accurately perceive what is being demonstrated.*

❋ **BALANCE:** *Balance is relative and measured, shall we say, by an individual's ability to faithfully demonstrate the various elements comprising his larger reality through the specific frameworks of form in which one has chosen to develop. When what one is demonstrating is faithful in intent and clarity with these elements and the larger reality, one experiences balance. And those interacting with this individual will experience his balance. One experiences imbalance when there is distortion between what one demonstrates through the form framework and the intent and clarity of the elements comprising the larger reality as well as the larger reality itself.*

If you truly look at what we are saying here, you will see that balance as a phenomenon is not an elusive state that only an exulted few can achieve. Balance is, in fact, inherent in all reality, in all life systems. Balance is defined by the many elements within any individual's reality. And it is the dominant state of being within any reality and any form system. It is also the state of being that links individual life systems to one another and to the larger whole. When one says that he is a child of the universe, what one is acknowledging is the relationship and link of his higher state of balance to the universe's state of balance. Whether one feels linked to or distant from this relationship, depends on the closeness or distance he creates within himself with respect to his larger personal state of balance—that dynamic which is part of his overall reality.

❋ **LIFE VITALITY:** *We have used this term frequently in these definitions and feel it would be useful to clarify what we mean. To understand life vitality, it is best to see it in relationship to order and organization. Order and organization are the physical structures that create the framework for form. In short, they define the walls. But we have included the dynamic of life vitality when we refer to form because one element of form is action, and it is life vitality that initiates and creates action. Nothing in form is stagnant. It is life vitality that gives to form its action. If the framework that is created from order and organization is incomplete, ineffective, deteriorating or being dismantled in an untimely manner, the dynamic of life vitality decreases within the overall form reality. This causes life movement to decrease accordingly, and is a movement towards a state of stagnation. It is the dynamic of vitality that gives life—movement—to any individual or object. Organization and order alone cannot do that. However, vitality without organization and order has no sense of* *purpose to its motion. It cannot function without organization and order. The three must be present and in balance with one another for there to be quality form expression. Nature, on the devic level, creates organization, order and life vitality in perfect balance. Nature, on the nature spirit level, maintains that balanced relationship as individual life units move through their evolutionary paces.*

We would like to illustrate what we are saying by focusing your attention on the soil-balancing process that improves and enhances the level of soil vitality. This process does not work directly with the soil's vitality level. Instead, it works with those elements of the soil that comprise its order and organization. The process shores up the physical structure of its order and organization. As a direct result, the soil begins to shift its form back to the original balance among organization, order and life vitality. As a consequence of this shift, the soil vitality level (the soil's life vitality) increases to its new state of balance. Those changes involve a comparable shift in the interaction and movement among all the different elements that comprise soil. This is why when someone observes change in a field that has had its soil balanced through the soil-balancing process, he sees greater efficiency between how the soil and plants interact. The action and movement in the soil have raised the soil's order and organizational structures back to the state (or nearer to the state) of the original devic balance of order, organization and life vitality.

❈ **GROUNDING**: *Quite simply, the word "grounded" is used to acknowledge full body/soul fusion or full matter/soul fusion. The word "grounding" refers to what must be accomplished or activated in order to both assure and stabilize body or matter/soul fusion. To be grounded refers to the state of being a fused body (matter)/soul unit. To achieve this unit fusion and to function fully as a fused unit is the primary goal one accepts when choosing to experience life within form. Functioning as a grounded body (matter)/soul unit is a goal on all levels and dimensions of form, whether the form can or cannot be perceived by the five senses.*

Nature plays two key roles in grounding. First, it is through and with nature that the grounding occurs. Nature, which organizes, orders and adds life vitality to create form, is what creates and maintains grounding. Secondly, the levels of nature know what is required to fuse the soul dynamic within form. Nature itself provides the best examples of body (matter)/soul fusion. Humans have recognized the form or matter existence of nature on the planet, but have only recently begun to understand that within all form there are fully functioning soul dynamics. On the other hand, humans acknowledge or concentrate on their personal soul dynamics but have little understanding as to how they, in order to be functional within form, must allow the soul to fuse with and operate through their form body. Humans do not see the examples and learn the lessons of the master teachers of body (matter)/soul fusion that surround them in all the kingdoms of nature. Humans also deny the fusion within themselves. The relative extent of this denial interferes proportionately with the quality and stabilization of the fusion.

❋ **INTENT**: *Intent refers to the conscious dynamic within all life that links life vitality with soul purpose and direction. When an individual uses free will to manipulate what he or she willfully desires instead of what is within the scope of higher soul purpose, then intent is combined with the manipulative power of free will and this combination is linked with life vitality. If you will recall, it is life vitality that adds action to order and organization. It both initiates and creates action. To maintain harmonious movement with soul purpose and direction, life vitality must be linked with the soul dynamic. This linkage occurs on two levels. One is unconscious, allowing for a natural patterning and rhythm of action through form that is consistent with soul purpose. As the body/soul fusion moves through its own evolutionary process as a functioning unit, it takes on a greater level of consciousness and an expanded level of awareness and knowing. As a result, the unconscious link between soul dynamic and life vitality takes on a new level of operation, thus shifting it into a state of consciousness. The shift is a gradual, step-by-step evolutionary process in itself. Intent is conscious awareness of soul purpose, what is required within the scope of form to achieve soul purpose, and how the two function as a unit. Consequently, when one wishes to express soul purpose, one need only consciously fuse this purpose with appropriate form and action. This act is what is referred to when one speaks of intent.*

Intent as a dynamic is an evolutionary process in itself and, as we have said, does not suddenly envelop one's entire life fully and completely. Intent is only gradually incorporated into one's everyday life. Therefore, one does not suddenly and immediately function within the full scope of the intent dynamic in those areas of life where intent is present. Intent as a dynamic is as broad a learning arena as life itself. And in the beginning, intent can often be confused with or intermingled with free will. However, as it is developed, it becomes the cutting edge of the body/soul unit and how it operates. Intent is the key to unlimited life within the scope of form.

❋ **INTUITION:** *Intuition, as it is popularly defined, relates to a sixth sense of operation. This is false. This is not a sixth sense. When individuals experience a phenomenon that they consider to be beyond their five senses, they tend to attribute this experience to another category, the sixth sense, and call it intuition. The fact is that these expanded experiences are processed through their five senses in an expanded manner.*

Intuition, in fact, is related to and linked with intent. It is the bridge between an individual's conscious body/soul fusion—that state which he knows and understands about the body/soul fusion and how it functions— and the individual's unconscious body/soul fusion. The intuition bridges the unconscious and the conscious. This enables what is known on the level of the unconscious body/soul fusion to be incorporated with and become a part of the conscious body/soul fusion. Intuition is the communication bridge between the two which makes it possible for the conscious body/soul unit to benefit from those aspects of the unconscious body/soul unit. This benefit results when the conscious unit opens to and moves through the lessons surrounding intent. Where intent is functioning fully, these two levels, the unconscious and the conscious, are no longer separate but have become one—the expanded conscious level. Consequently, there is then no need for the bridge known as intuition.

However, lest you think otherwise, intent is not considered greater than intuition; rather, they are two excellent tools utilized equally by the highest developed souls functioning within form. We say this to caution those who read this not to think intent is "greater" than intuition and to be aimed for at the exclusion of intuition. Evolution as seen from the highest perspective is endless. Therefore, discovery of all there is to know about both intuition and intent is endless. For all practical purposes, an individual can safely consider that there will never be a time in which the development of intent will be such that the need for and development of intuition will be unnecessary. As we have said, the highest souls who function to the fullest within the scope of form do so with an equal development and expansion of both intent and intuition.

Moving on to the energy processes: Chapter 18 of the *Perelandra Garden Workbook* introduced three energy processes to be used in conjunction with nature in the garden and in agriculture in general. They are the Energy Cleansing Process, the Battle Energy Release Process and the Soil Balancing Process. Since publishing the *Workbook*, nature has focused on and expanded the work at Perelandra around co-creative, cooperative energy work. This has had such an astounding impact on the garden and on how I approach the garden that I am convinced that we are now to expand our understanding of working co-creatively with nature in a two-prong approach.

The first seventeen chapters of the *Workbook* describe the first prong. They lay the foundation of co-creative gardening and farming by explaining to and instructing us in what I now call the "environmental" processes. We learn about working with nature to locate a garden properly, to design it well and to plan its rows, as well as what gets planted in those rows in a manner that encourages strength. We learn how to work with nature to discern what fertilizers are needed and how much, as well as how to incorporate animals and insects into the garden balance. All these processes focus on incorporating nature intelligences in how we work, what tools we choose, what seeds we select, where we put them and what planting rhythm we use. We ask nature to give us input around these very familiar practices so that we can upgrade and put into balance what we are already doing.

Chapter 18 of the *Workbook* introduces the second prong and, along with it, a change in our work with nature intelligences. The three energy processes are not familiar gardening and farming practices either in concept or in approach. They are designed to allow us to work with nature on a level that is very different from finding out what fertilizers are needed and how much. In fact, these energy processes open a door to a new world in which we begin to discover that the balance and health of a garden and, for that matter, of all natural form are more complex than just finding out what fertilizer is needed. A balanced garden or farm environment must also include balanced energy and vitality. And this introduces us to the many elements of a balanced garden or farm that we can't see—the energy elements.

My work with nature since 1987 has convinced me that environmental processes and energy processes may be very different in concept, but they are equal in importance. To work with nature co-creatively through the environmental processes but ignore energy processes would be to exclude half of the picture. We would, in effect, be tying one of our hands and one of nature's hands behind our respective backs.

To understand why we need so many co-creative processes as we work with nature to develop a balanced and healthy garden or farm, it is important to understand that a garden or farm is not a natural nature environment. Both are created and developed by human beings. We got tired of all that hunting, foraging and moving around a long time ago and came up with the creative idea of centralizing everything we need for food survival in one convenient spot. We cannot go out into the wild, if there is such a thing left, and expect to find a vegetable garden or a family farm. We can find things to eat in the wild, but that would be foraging and hunting, not gardening and farming. So from the very beginning of gardening, we humans imposed our idea of convenient order and organization onto nature. Either we lost our understanding of what we did when we implemented the garden concept, or we never understood what we did and assumed that a garden or farm inherently has a nature balance. It does not. The difficulty we have had over the centuries in discovering an approach or method that would assure good balance and, at the same time, good production bears this out.

What we have with a garden or farm (or any land management situation) is our need and our ideas about how to satisfy that need superimposed on top of nature. I don't for a minute want you to think that I am suggesting that we ditch the gardening and farming approach and return to hunting and foraging. We'd probably all starve to death. And I have never, in all of my work with nature intelligences, felt that nature wanted us to ditch these things. But what we *do* need to understand is that it is essential for us to work co-creatively and cooperatively with nature to develop a system and methods that will satisfy our practical needs as well as nature's need to strike a balance within any given environment. The two go hand in hand. The present global ecological disaster gives us ample evidence of what happens when we focus on our needs at the cost of nature's needs.

In trying to understand what is going on at Perelandra, people have assumed that nature has all the answers and all I have to do is listen and implement what they are saying. The result, these people reason, is perfection. Sometimes people think my cabbages smile and my rabbits sing arias. And, of course, my vegetables should each weigh no less than forty pounds. I bring all of this up because to maintain such myths is to completely misconstrue what is going on at Perelandra. That would do a disservice to those of you who are using the co-creative methods. These myths take us in a direction that is 180 degrees from the reality of what is happening when we work co-creatively with nature. In the myth, we humans are children who are told by our nature parents precisely what we are to do if we wish to have perfection. It's a myth that inspires laziness on our part. We relinquish all our responsibilities as intelligent humans capable of functioning intelligently.

For us to work co-creatively with nature, we must work in *partnership* with nature. We must also understand that although nature fully knows the dynamics and relationship of energy to form, new processes must be developed when those dynamics are taken out of the natural arena and applied in new ways. An example is the garden. Plants grow in a natural arena. In the wild, nature knows how to apply the principles of energy and form that will create a balanced environment which will enhance all elements that are part of that environment. As I already pointed out, a garden does not grow in the wild. By creating gardens and farms, we humans defined new environments with new directions and purposes. We now need to allow nature the opportunity to develop new processes that are applicable to the new environment and that encompass the universal principles of energy and form. However, for the sake of *our* growth, understanding and overall efficiency in this situation, we need to work with nature *in partnership*. If we are to initiate new purpose and direction, new needs and goals and, at the same time, acquire from nature the means to achieve these objectives, we must work with nature directly and in partnership for good, solid, balanced development.

Since 1976, Perelandra has been dedicated to working with nature in partnership, developing the processes necessary for establishing and maintaining the partnership, and developing the processes necessary for extending that partnership into the various environmental arenas in which humans and nature must work together to create. The environmental processes in the *Workbook* and the energy processes presented in *Workbook II* are the result of that partnership. They are designed to address the various issues that we and nature face in any environmental situation in which humans and nature impact upon one another. By definition, this impact implies that a partnership is needed and new processes must be applied.

OVERLIGHTING DEVA OF PERELANDRA

We would like to add our thoughts to what Machaelle has already said. With the introduction and implementation of the various co-creative energy processes coming from the work at Perelandra, we of nature feel that, indeed, we are entering a new stage in the ever-growing partnership that is being established between us and you. As Machaelle has explained, it is important that what we already know and have established as natural process within the arena of nature in the wild be appropriately modified, expanded and applied in the vast number of arenas where humans and nature have the opportunity to meet in partnership.

Where there is partnership or where there is a need for partnership, we of nature will not automatically function as if a partnership is already formed and operating. Where man and nature come together, there must be **conscious** *partnership. We will not assume both roles of a partnership and automatically give to humans the fruits of what would have resulted had* *there been a partnership. In short, without the partnership, nature will function in a manner that will best suit that which is needed for environmental balance **as we know it**. We will not automatically accommodate human need and desire. We will strive for environmental balance and assume that humans will modify their needs and desires accordingly. We in nature cannot take on the human role and supply human insight into the partnership. Consequently, where there is need for partnership—which, quite frankly, is in every endeavor of humans on Earth—there must be partnership in order for the new processes to be both developed and implemented.*

And this leads us to the next point: Just as we will not assume the role of the human in partnership when developing necessary processes, we will also not assume the full responsibility of implementing those processes when partnership is the intent. This is why we establish co-creative processes with both humans and nature in mind. The co-creative process maintains in its structure the human role and nature's role. One does not do the other's job. Only when nature is functioning within its own arena, an arena in which humans do not impact, is it appropriate for us to function as sole operators within the universal laws of matter and spirit, form and energy.

It is true that we of nature are the creators and initiators of all order, organization and life vitality within the form reality. However, in areas of partnership, we do not supersede human intent with that which we know or that which we create. It is the human intent in this partnership around which we create nature's order, organization and life vitality.

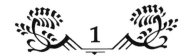

Creating and Working
in a Coning

For the environmental processes, we generally work with one specific nature intelligence at a time in order to get the information we need. For example, we'll work with the deva of a garden to find out what seeds are to be planted in what rows. We'll work with the Deva of Soil to get information regarding fertilizers. For the energy processes, we need to expand from working with one nature intelligence at a time to working with a team called a "coning."

A coning is a balanced vortex of conscious energy. The simple way to explain a coning is to say that it is a conference call. It is as simple to create and activate a coning as it is to connect with a single nature intelligence. But, with a coning, we are working with more than one intelligence simultaneously.

The reason a coning is needed for energy-process work is because of the greater stability, clarity and balance it offers over working with one nature intelligence. When getting environmental information as described in the *Workbook*, it is efficient and appropriate to work with the one intelligence involved. A coning is unnecessary. However, with the energy processes, we are working with larger concepts involving many different facets and levels of nature.

Consequently, it is far better to work in a team comprised of all involved in the area we are focused on.

A coning, by nature, has a high degree of protection built into it. Because of the larger scope of the work in the energy processes, it is important to define exactly who and what are involved in that work. All others are excluded by the mere fact that they have not been activated. In essence, a coning creates not only the team but also the room in which the team is meeting. It is important, when activating a coning, to discern between those team members who are a part of the work to be done and others who are not involved. The coning is created and activated by us—the human team member. Only those with whom we seek connection will be included. Members will not "slide" in and out of a coning on their own. This adds to the exceptional degree of protection contained within the coning.

I have said that a coning also offers balance and clarity. A friend of mine who began to use a coning whenever she did multilevel healing work was quite impressed at the difference the coning made in both the quality of her work and the process she went through during her work. She said that when she began to do her work while "in coning," she felt as if she was sitting in a beautiful, sunlit room with the windows open and a lovely warm breeze softly blowing in. Before she learned to use a coning, she would just "connect in" with various "helpers." She said it was as if she was sitting in a room with no windows and struggling to get a full breath of air. What she was describing was the contrast in what she felt from the balance and clarity the coning gave her.

Any combination of team members can be activated for the

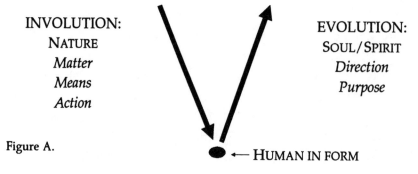

INVOLUTION:
NATURE
Matter
Means
Action

EVOLUTION:
SOUL/SPIRIT
Direction
Purpose

Figure A.

← HUMAN IN FORM

purpose of simultaneous input. But this does not constitute a con-ing. A true coning has balance built into it. By this I mean a balance between nature and the human soul. In order for us to experience anything fully, we must perceive it in a balanced state; i.e., it must have an equal reflection of the soul or spirit dynamics (evolution) combined with an equal reflection of the form/nature dynamics (in-volution). I see this balance in the shape of a V. (See Figure A.)

For anything to function well in form, it must have within it a balance between the involution dynamics and the evolution dynamics, or nature and spirit. The extent to which we achieve balance between the involution and evolution dynamics depends on our willingness to allow nature to partner with us. A focus that is primarily involutionary results in a person or situation that is form-oriented with little or no purpose or direction. This is essentially form and movement without soul or spirit. A focus that is primarily fixed on evolution results in an airy-fairy situation or person that has no effective order or organization and no means of action for implementation. To have soul and spirit effectively, efficiently and fully activated into form and action, one must have a balance be-tween involution and evolution.

A coning is set up for the purpose of activating a team for specific work—in this case, the energy processes. It is therefore important, for the successful completion of the work, that a balance be main-tained between the involution dynamics and the evolution dynamics within the coning itself. We do this by setting up a basic coning, which I call the "4-point coning," that lays a balanced in-volution/evolution foundation. (See Figure B.)

The 4-point coning, as a foundation, maintains the necessary

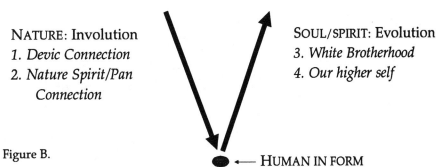

NATURE: Involution
1. *Devic Connection*
2. *Nature Spirit/Pan
Connection*

SOUL/SPIRIT: Evolution
3. *White Brotherhood*
4. *Our higher self*

Figure B.

⬤ ← HUMAN IN FORM

balance between (a) involution or nature, through its connection with the devic and nature spirit levels and (b) evolution, through its connection with the White Brotherhood level and the higher self of the person or persons working in the coning. We human souls supply the evolutionary dynamic only. We cannot supply the involutionary dynamic.

A note about the White Brotherhood: The White Brotherhood is a large group of highly evolved souls who are dedicated to assisting the evolutionary process of moving universal reality, principles, laws and patterns through all planes and levels of form. They hold the major patterning and rhythms being utilized for the shift we are all going through from the Piscean to the Aquarian era. They are part of a balanced coning because they support and assist in assuring that any work conducted from the coning maintains its forward motion and its connection to the new Aquarian dynamics. For the purpose of a coning, we do not need to link with an individual in the White Brotherhood. In fact, it is preferred that we simply link the coning with the White Brotherhood *generally*, as if we were calling into their "office building" but not being connected to a specific office. A general connection to this level assures that the evolutionary dynamic in the coning is consistent with the intent and direction of the new Aquarian shift.

We include our higher self in the coning to assure that all the work done is compatible with our higher direction and purpose. This input is made by us automatically by the mere fact that our higher self is linked into the coning.

The devic connection assures that the work being done in coning maintains an overall integrity with nature's design and direction in the area in which we are working.

The nature spirit level is connected through Pan. We do this because all nature spirits except Pan are regional, and rather than try to figure out which nature spirit or groups of nature spirits are involved in the work we wish to do, we work with Pan—the one nature spirit who is universal in dynamic and is involved in all of the nature spirit activities. If one were to look at the nature spirits bureaucratically, one could say that Pan is their chief executive officer. To work with Pan is to maintain consistency in the coning and to give assurance that the nature spirit activity and input is fully covered at all times.

NOTE: In order to do the energy processes described in this book, you need to know how to do kinesiology. Kinesiology is the fancy word for muscle testing and is explained fully in appendix A in this book and in the *Workbook* (chapter 2). All the testing and verification work that are referred to throughout the energy process steps are done by kinesiology.

Soil kits are also needed, and I have included information about this in appendix B.

Flower essences are used in most of the processes, as well as for balancing and stabilizing ourselves as we do the processes. Flower essences and how to use them are described in chapter 16 of the *Workbook* and appendix C in this book. They are also described in detail in the book, *Flower Essences*.

To do the environmental processes described in the *Workbook*, I am assuming that you have learned to kinesiology test. Using flower essences and the soil kit also are based on kinesiology. Therefore, it will be comparatively easy to include them in your gardening and agricultural tools if you haven't already done so. For those of you who are using the environmental processes in the *Workbook*, you will see that incorporating flower essences and the soil kit into your work will be just like working more lists.

IMPORTANT: To keep you from getting frustrated, I suggest that you completely read this chapter and chapter 2 before opening a 4-point coning or doing the three *Workbook* energy processes in chapter 2. There are balancing and stabilizing steps listed in these processes that won't make much sense until you read the Soil Balancing and Stabilizing section in chapter 2. After chapter 2, you will have all the background information you'll need to do each process once you've read it.

STEPS FOR OPENING A 4-POINT CONING

Have your flower essences and soil balancing kit handy.

1. State:

     I wish to open a coning.

2. Link with each appropriate member of the coning individually:
     a) the specific deva(s) involved
     b) Pan
     c) the White Brotherhood—State:

          I'd like to be connected with the White Brotherhood.
     d) your higher self—State:

          I'd like to be connected with my higher self.

If you do not feel a connection occur, that's fine. Allow about 10 seconds for the connection to occur, just as you would when linking with a deva or nature spirit individually for the environmental processes. Then verify your connection (using kinesiology) before going on to the next connection.

3. Balance and stabilize the coning. Ask:

     What balancers are needed for the coning? (Test your soil kit balancers.)

Work with Pan to shift the balancers that tested positive into the coning just as you would work with Pan to shift balancers into soil. Then ask:

     What stabilizers are needed for the coning? (Test your flower essences.)

Again work with Pan to shift the essences that tested positive into the coning.

(Remember, to fully understand what is done for this step, you'll need to read the section on Soil Balancing and Stabilizing.)

NOTE: I have found that although a coning is quite stable in itself, this stability is enhanced if the coning is balanced and stabilized. In this case, we are not working with a specific area of soil. Rather, we are balancing and stabilizing the physical reality of the coning as it relates to the natural environment in which it has been activated. I have found that I operate more smoothly in a balanced and stabilized coning than I do in a regular coning.

4. Test yourself for flower essences to make sure that the process of activating a coning did not affect your balance. Take any essences you tested positive for. You will not need to do a dosage test at this time for these essences because they are needed for one time only, while you are in the coning. To test yourself for essences, ask:
   Do I need any flower essences? (Test)
If no, continue with the coning steps. If yes, test the essences.

5. Do the process or work you desire.

6. When the work or process is completed, thank your team for its assistance and close down or dismantle the coning. *This is important.* You do this simply by focusing on each member of the coning separately, thanking that member, and asking to be disconnected. Then verify that you are disconnected from each member using kinesiology.

7. Test yourself for flower essences again, just to be sure that you held your balance once the coning work was complete. Take the essences that tested positive and, this time, *check for dosage* to see if you will need to take the essence(s) more than one time.

If you have difficulty closing down the coning and keep getting a negative kinesiological response to the question, "Am I disconnected from _____?", it is simply because you have temporarily lost your focus on what you are doing. No member of the coning is going to resist a disconnection any more than a member would resist a connection. You are the one in command of the creation, activation and dismantling of the coning. All you need to do when having a little trouble closing down is refocus yourself on what you are doing, request a disconnection again and test to verify the disconnection. This time you will receive a positive verification.

The above steps are for opening a 4-point coning. There will be times when you will need to work with more than four team members. For example, with some work you will need the devas both of a garden and of soil. Also, there will be times when you will want to do an energy process with others (people, that is!). Once the 4-point coning is open and activated, your stabilizing foundation is laid and you may add any number of team members to that foundation. So, if you are working with a process that requires the Deva of Soil to be present, and two friends, Sally and Herbert, are participating with you during the process, you would:

1. Open the 4-point coning.

2. Ask to be linked with the Deva of Soil.

*You will function as the
leader when other people are
included in the coning and,
as leader, you will do all the
testing.*

3. Ask that Sally's higher self be connected with the coning. Test to verify this connection.

4. Ask that Herbert's higher self be connected with the coning. Test to verify the connection.

5. Balance and stabilize the coning. Then test Sally, Herbert and yourself for flower essences. Take the essences needed, one time only.

6. Do the process as you normally would, including Sally and Herbert in the process wherever appropriate. Be careful not to modify or alter the steps in any way in an effort to include them.

7. Once the work is complete, thank the coning team and dismantle the coning by asking to be disconnected with:
Sally's higher self
Herbert's higher self
Deva of Soil
Then, the 4-point coning:
    a) All devic connections, one at a time
    b) Nature Spirit/Pan Connection
    c) White Brotherhood
    d) Our higher self
Test after each disconnection to make sure it has occurred.

8. Test Sally, Herbert and yourself again for flower essences. Take those essences and check for dosage for each person to see if the essences need to be taken more than one time.

Some Important Points to Remember about a Coning

1. You may include as many members in your team as you like and maintain involution/evolution balance as long as you begin with the 4-point coning as your foundation. However, it is best to include *only* those who are directly related to the work being done. Some people get a little crazy about coning activation and add forty-two members who might possibly be involved or would like to be involved, maybe. If you do, you no longer have a tight, cohesive team. You now have a mob coning instead.

I urge you to resist activating a mob coning for two reasons.

a) It is totally unnecessary and does not strengthen or enhance a coning in any way.

b) *You,* as the initiator and activator of the coning, will feel a substantial physical drain as you try to hold a coning with an unnecessary number of members present throughout the time it takes to do a process. A coning, although invisible, is a physical energy reality that will interact with you. It may require of you the same amount of output as you would expend if you were trying to hold a deep conversation with six people in the middle of the New York Stock Exchange on Friday afternoon. You are going to feel exhausted from this kind of overload. So, the key to "good coning-building" is to be precise about who you request to be on the team. Each member should have an integral role in the work to be done.

You will need only the one connection to the White Brotherhood and the one connection to the nature spirit level with Pan. The devic level is represented by the deva of the area you are working with (in the 4-point coning) and any other deva who is directly involved in the process you are working with. For the energy processes I am giving you in this book, I will include a list of who is to be linked into the coning. The other rule of thumb about coning members is that you must include the higher self of anyone who is physically present during the work.

2. Because working in a coning is a physical phenomenon for us, we need to address some basic physical needs.

a) We should not work in a coning for more than *one hour at a time.* This is especially true in the beginning when we are getting used to working with and in a coning. Your body needs time to adjust to this new dynamic. For the energy processes, this amount of time will more than cover the time needed for any one process and will usually give you enough time to do two or three processes, if necessary. If you need to do three energy processes and cannot do them back to back within the one-hour time frame, close down the coning after one of the processes and continue with the others later that day or the next day.

b) Activating, working with and dismantling a coning require sharp focus on our part. As a result, we may experience a protein drain. You will know you are experiencing such a drain if you come out of the coning and are suddenly attacked with a galloping case of the munchies. Oftentimes, we translate a protein drain into a desire for sweets. I have nothing against a great piece of chocolate from time to time. But in this case, you need protein to compensate for the drain. Then eat your chocolate.

HINT: Have a bag of nuts with you while you are in coning and occasionally down a few. This will avoid or minimize the protein drain while you are in the coning.

Also, I find that while in the coning, I do not perceive the protein drain or any hunger. They don't register until after I close down the coning. So I suggest that, if you are not hungry during the coning, don't let that fool you. Still have your supply of nuts handy and eat a few throughout the session.

3. If you need to take a break during a coning session, do not close the coning and then re-open it. Just tell your team that you need a break for fifteen minutes or a half-hour or whatever (don't make it a vacation). They will automatically shift the coning into what I call the "at-rest position." You may feel the intensity of the coning back off a bit when this shift occurs. It will take all of about five seconds. Then have your break. When you are ready to resume, announce that your break is over and the coning will automatically shift back into its previous connection and intensity.

4. Don't get into the habit of activating conings indiscriminately. They are to be used for interlevel work and process and not for prediction-type information. Your coning members are functioning

in a team-like dynamic with you and do not wish to be asked to function in areas where your common sense should be the dominant factor. Opening a coning to ask if you should go on a specific vacation or if it would be good for you to invest money in a certain stock is not appropriate. As far as your team is concerned, such decisions are best left to your common sense and intelligence.

There is something else I would like to explain. Some people use kinesiology to discern issues about themselves. For example, they may wish to know if they are to take a certain vitamin or if it would strengthen or weaken them to wear a certain color to a certain business meeting. These are questions that can be accurately answered using kinesiology and should not be addressed to a coning. They are to be directed to the individual who wants that information. If I want to know whether I should wear yellow or red for a special occasion in order to enhance my strength and balance, I already have the answer within myself. Our higher self functions much like the devic level in nature in that it contains all the information around the patterns, plans, directions, rhythms and designs we need in order to operate. So, if I wish to know something about a color, I access that higher level of myself (the higher self) and ask.

(To connect with the higher self, all one needs to do is state: "I wish to be connected to my higher self." Then test to verify the connection. Ask the questions you wish, and then close the connection once you are finished. You do not, in closing that connection, sever yourself from your higher self. However, it is essential that you close this *special* connection because it requires energy and focus for you to maintain it. If it is not closed, it will drain your energy.)

I also suggest that you limit the questions to issues that pertain to the present. Information about the future is reliable only if all issues and elements involved remain *exactly* the same as they were when you asked your questions. In a changing world populated by people with active free wills, this never happens. By the time you get to a future point in time, all issues and elements will most likely have changed perspective and position. Therefore your answers about what to do will also need to change. In short, I'm suggesting that it's a waste of time and a crap shoot to try to see into the future.

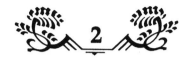

The *Workbook* Energy Processes

The Energy Cleansing Process, Battle Energy Release Process and the Soil Balancing Process are already described in the *Workbook*, so I won't repeat the more lengthy descriptions here. However, I am outlining the steps for each because they are often referred to when energy process work is needed. As a threesome, they are the first energy processes used when working with any land or within any environment. Right off the bat, before we do any planning or work with a piece of land, one should test for the need to do these three processes *before* proceeding with other energy processes.

In fact, once a partnership is formed with nature and the site for a garden is located, it would be best to test for the need to do these three processes before proceeding with the environmental planning sessions described in the *Workbook*. I did not suggest this order in the *Workbook* because, at the time, I felt it is important that a person, especially one new to the co-creative method, learn how to work with nature through the environmental processes before being faced with the more complex energy processes.

When beginning the co-creative process on a piece of land, you most likely will find that the land needs all three energy processes: the Energy Cleansing Process, Battle Energy Release Process and the

Soil Balancing and Stabilizing Process. Consider it a major sweeping out. The best way to handle this is to open a 4-point coning and do all three processes back to back. They are designed to link together well this way. The Energy Cleansing Process releases the surface emotional energy present in the area and prepares for the deeper releases brought about by the Battle Energy Release Process. Then it is important to move right into the Soil Balancing and Stabilization Process to strengthen, balance and stabilize the land. All three processes operate as a package and lay the foundation for any work, environmental or energy, that will follow.

After these three processes have been done for a specific environment, like a garden or a field, the Battle Energy Release Process need not be done again. However, from time to time, you will probably have to repeat the Energy Cleansing and Soil Balancing and Stabilization Processes back to back. Kinesiology can tell you whether that is necessary and, if so, when. For example, each year at the beginning of the spring planting cycle, I test to see whether I should do these two processes for the Perelandra garden environment. I have always gotten a yes. It's like sweeping out debris that may have become a part of the garden environment over the winter. So I begin my work in the garden with these two processes and move on to other energy processes from there. Also, you will find as we go on that there will be some energy processes that will be set up by first doing either these three processes as a package or the Energy Cleansing and Soil Balancing and Stabilizing Processes together before proceeding with the additional energy process.

I am outlining below an abbreviated version of the steps for each of the three processes, since the processes themselves are fully described in the *Workbook*. I assume that you have read the *Workbook* and used the more expanded version of the steps in it. The abbreviated steps listed below will serve as a quick reference as you work with these processes in conjunction with other energy processes in this paper. I have added to the steps below the steps for balancing yourself with essences as well as balancing and stabilizing the coning and the work. This is because of the additional support these three steps give.

ENERGY CLEANSING PROCESS

THE WORKBOOK
ENERGY PROCESSES
Energy Cleansing
Battle Energy Release
Soil Balancing & Stabilizing

1. Choose and diagram the area to be cleansed. Place the diagram in front of you during the process. Have your flower essences and soil balancing kit handy.

2. Prepare yourself for doing the process. Relax and focus.

3. Open a 4-point coning. Balance and stabilize the coning. Check yourself for essences.

The deva will be the overlighting deva of the land you are working with. State:

> I would like to be connected with the overlighting deva of this land.

You need not have a formal devic name in mind to make this connection. Just refer to it as the overlighting deva of the land you are working with.

For complete understanding of how to work with the soil balancing kit and flower essences, you'll need to read the Soil Balancing and Stabilizing section of this chapter. Also, see appendix B for more information on the soil balancing kit and appendix C for general information and ordering information on flower essences.

4. See a bright white beam of light above your head. This is the light of the christ (the term traditionally used to describe the *evolutionary dynamic* contained within us all, which does not refer to the religious figure, Jesus Christ). See the light rays from this beam move down toward you and totally envelop you in white light. State to yourself or aloud:

> I ask that the light of the christ aid me so that what I am about to do will be for the highest good. I ask that this light help me in transmuting the ungrounded emotional energies released by us humans and that I be protected fully during this process. I welcome your presence and thank you for your help.

5. See a second beam of light, a green light—the light of nature (the *involutionary dynamic* contained within us all). See the light totally envelop you, commingling with the white light. State:

> I ask that the light of nature aid me in releasing and collecting the energies absorbed by the nature kingdoms, tangible and intangible, animate and inanimate. I also ask that the light of nature aid me so that what I am about to do is for the

HINT: If you find it cumbersome to read the process steps while trying to do them at the same time, just tape record the steps for yourself. Remember to leave time between each step for doing it.

highest good. I welcome your presence and thank you for your help.

6. State:

I ask that any inappropriate, stagnant, darkened or ungrounded energies release from the intended area. I request this in *gentleness and love*, knowing that the cleansing and transmutation process I am about to be a part of is a process of life, of evolution—and not negation.

7. Visualize the area to be cleansed.

8. Visualize a thin white sheet of light forming five feet *below* the lowest point of your area. Allow the outside edges of the sheet to extend five feet *beyond* the outside boundary of the area.

9. Ask that the light of the christ and the light of nature join you as together you *slowly* move the sheet up and through the area to be cleansed. Allow the sheet to rise five feet *above* the highest point of the area you are cleansing.

10. Carefully gather the edges of the sheet, through the use of your visualization, forming a bundle of white light that totally encloses the collected, darkened energies. To the left of the bundle, see the gold thread from the light of the christ. Tie the bundle closed with this thread. To the right of the sheet, see the gold thread from the light of nature and tie it also around the top of the bundle along with the first thread.

11. State:

I now release the bundle to the light of the christ and the light of nature so that the energies that have been released can be moved on to their next higher level for transmutation and the continuation of their own evolutionary process.

Watch the bundle lift. Just watch and do not try to determine where the next higher level is.

12. Return your focus to the now-cleansed area. Observe the area.

13. Shift your focus to your breathing, focusing on your body as you inhale and exhale three or four times.

14. Recognize the various energies that assisted during this process: the white light of the christ, the green light of nature, the white sheet, the two gold threads and the energies that were released.

15. Return your focus to the room or environment around you.

16. Balance and stabilize the work that was just completed in this process. Ask:

> What balancers are needed for this energy cleansing? (Test your soil kit.)

Work with Pan to shift the balancers into the area impacted by the Energy Cleansing Process.

Then ask:

> What stabilizers are needed for this energy cleansing? (Test the flower essences.)

Again, work with Pan to shift the stabilizers into the area impacted by the process.

17. If you are not doing another energy process now, thank the team, *close the 4-point coning* and test yourself for essences and dosage. If you are going on, keep the same coning activated and simply move on to the next process.

BATTLE ENERGY RELEASE PROCESS

1. If you do not have a coning already activated, open a 4-point coning. The deva to be connected with will be the overlighting deva of the land you are working with. Balance and stabilize the coning. Check yourself for essences.

You will need your flower essences and soil balancing kit for this.

2. State that you present yourself as a representative of mankind who has come to nature in the spirit of care, concern, love and co-creativity to help release any battle energies held by nature, and to facilitate that process.

3. **The release:** Ask nature to now release all the battle energies *with gentleness and ease*, and request that the released energy gather as an energy cloud above the land area.

Watch or feel the release. This will take anywhere from a few minutes to a half-hour. When you sense that the release is complete, kinesiology test to verify.

4. When the release is complete, request that the released energy that has gathered as an energy cloud over the land now move to its next higher level within the universe. (Do not try to determine where that might be.)

5. Spend a moment noticing the changes and sensations you might be feeling from the land. This serves to fully ground the completed process.

6. Balance and stabilize the work you have just completed. Use the same steps you used when balancing and stabilizing the Energy Cleansing Process work. (See step 16.)

7. *Close the coning* after thanking the team, and check yourself for essences and dosage, unless you are going on immediately to the next process.

SOIL BALANCING AND STABILIZING PROCESS

Since introducing this process in the *Workbook,* I have found that its use is greatly expanded from what I originally thought. In the beginning, I used it as a process by itself. Then nature and I found that it was advantageous to work the Energy Cleansing Process, the Battle Energy Release Process and the Soil Balancing Process (its original name) together as a unit.

Then the Soil Balancing Process expanded in two more ways. 1) The flower essences were added to the process and used to *stabilize* the balancing already accomplished in the process. Consequently, the name of the process changed to the Soil Balancing and Stabilizing Process. 2) We discovered that by balancing and stabilizing *every* energy process, we greatly strengthened, protected and enhanced the work done in the process. To do this, once the energy process was completed, I would balance the area I was working with, using the soil balancers in the kit (lime, greensand, rock phosphate, etc.) and stabilize that area, using the flower essences.

To fully appreciate the importance of the Soil Balancing and Stabilizing Process, it is helpful to understand something about form and nature's relationship to form. I'll therefore repeat excerpts from the Co-Creative Definitions to remind you what nature means when it refers to form, nature and life vitality.

❀ FORM: *We consider reality to be in the form state when there is organization, order and life vitality combined with a state of consciousness.*

❀ NATURE: *Nature comprises all form on all levels and dimensions and is responsible for and creates all of form's order, organization and life vitality. Nature is the conscious reality that supplies order, organization and life vitality for moving soul-oriented consciousness into any dimension or level of form. Nature is form's order, organization and life vitality.*

❀ LIFE VITALITY: *To understand life vitality, it is best to see it in relationship to order and organization. Order and organization are the physical structures that create form framework. In short, they define the walls. But we have included the dynamic of life vitality that initiates and creates action. Nothing in form is stagnant. It is life vitality that gives to form its action. If the framework that is created from order and organization is incomplete, ineffective, deteriorating or being dismantled in an untimely manner, the dynamic of life vitality decreases within the overall form reality, thus causing life movement to decrease accordingly. There is a movement towards a state of stagnation. It is the dynamic of vitality that gives life—movement—to any individual or object. Organization and order alone cannot do this. However, vitality without corresponding organization and order has no sense of purpose to its motion. It cannot function without organization and order. The three must be present and in balance with one another in order for there to be quality form expression. Nature, on the devic level, creates organization, order and life vitality in perfect balance. Nature, on the nature spirit level, maintains that balanced relationship as individual life units move through their evolutionary paces.*

We would like to illustrate what we are saying by focusing your attention on the soil-balancing process that improves and enhances the level of soil vitality. This process does not work directly with the soil's vitality level. Instead, it works with those elements of the soil that comprise its order and organization. The process shores up the physical structure of its order and organization. As a direct result, the soil begins its shift back to its original form balance among organization, order and life vitality, and as a consequence of this shift, the soil vitality level (the soil's life vitality) automatically increases to its new state of balance. When this occurs, there is a comparable shift in the interaction and movement among all the different elements that comprise soil. This is why when someone observes change in a field that has had its soil balanced through the soil-balancing process, he sees greater efficiency in the interaction between the soil and the plants. The dynamic of action and movement in the soil has been raised by returning the soil's order and organizational structures back to the state (or nearer to the state) of the original devic order, organization and life vitality balance.

Now to fill you in on some of its history since this process was introduced in the *Workbook*.

In December, 1988, I received a letter from a Canadian soil scientist requesting that I send him a soil sample from the Perelandra garden and another (control) sample from the field surrounding the garden so that he could get an idea of the condition of the soil my garden started with. He was involved with soil testing using radionics, and he suspected that the Perelandra garden soil sample might provide him with some interesting information. I sent him the sample, and on February 5, 1989, I received a letter from him saying that the control sample (field soil) vitality measured 220 and the Perelandra garden soil vitality measured (using radionics) 470. He then went on to explain: "The analysis that I undertook using my radionic machine is enclosed. Basically what was found was that the Perelandra soil has the highest energy readings of any soil sample that I have tested to date. To explain what the numbers on the sheet mean, the Vitality is the overall energy level of the soil . . . an average for most soils is 200-300." He further explained that prior to getting the *Workbook*, he had been using the radionics method to raise soil vitality, which took 3-4 days to accomplish. With the Soil Balancing Process, he was able to raise the vitality level of the soil in 2-3 hours.

Regarding the wisdom of working with nature in these matters, he said in another letter: "I have been doing research on the effect of flower essence combinations that are chosen according to the methods explained in your book [the *Workbook*]. The flower essences chosen by the devas always raise the general vitality reading the highest of any possible combination."

The soil scientist and I continued working with understanding soil vitality and its relationship to the energy processes for a year and a half. We discovered that soil vitality has an annual rhythm that reaches its peak in the summer at the summer solstice and hits its lowest point in the fall at the fall equinox. It then levels off throughout the winter and begins to rise again in late winter to the spring equinox.

In the spring of 1989, the soil scientist began a new garden in a new location he had just moved to. He wrote me a letter just after doing the Perelandra vitality readings for the summer solstice, saying that the Perelandra garden was now at a level of 530-540. Then he said:

> . . . My garden soil started this spring with a vitality reading of 220 and currently is 530. During this time [May to July] there have been 2 soil balancings on the garden as well as 1 atmospheric balancing. Also there have been several physical treatments on the soil using the best that I as a soil scientist and the Deva of Soil can muster . . . One thing that I have noticed is the almost ethereal quality of our vegetables compared to the store-bought ones. Watching the garden unfold this year has been a real adventure since the majority of activities of the garden given by the devas were different than I normally would have expected based on my experience . . .

One of the things that impressed and excited me about what this scientist was saying was that by using the processes set up by nature, he was able to shift the vitality level of his soil from 220 to 530 in just two months.

So, the Soil Balancing and Stabilizing Process is now used in three ways: (a) to balance and stabilize a coning, (b) to raise the vitality level of any given area and (c) to balance and stabilize any area right after it has been shifted and changed due to any of the energy processes.

During this research, we were working with soil to a depth of at least five feet. It would be impossible, short of destroying the soil structure, to add balancers and stabilizers to that depth. (When we fertilize, we work only with the top 6-8 inches of soil, which is far more easily accessible.) So, to do the process, we rely on nature spirits—Pan, in this case—to assist us in distributing the balancers and stabilizers appropriately. We supply a seed amount (about 1/8 teaspoon) of the balancers and a drop of each of the stabilizers. Pan expands the seed amounts of the energies to whatever amounts are needed by the soil, and transfers those energies to appropriate depths in the soil. Once the energies are seated in the soil, Pan shifts them back to appropriate form (not solid matter), and thereby makes them accessible to and a part of the total soil environment.

IMPORTANT: This process does not replace the fertilizing processes described in Chapter 9 of the *Workbook*, nor does it replace the need for fertilizing in general. The Soil Balancing and Stabilizing Process impacts the soil's vitality and not its physical fertilizer levels. However, when you use the Soil Balancing and Stabilizing Process, you will find that the soil will test for fewer fertilizer needs. This is because the soil balancing and stabilizing have improved the soil vitality, which has then allowed for more efficient interaction between plants and their surrounding soil. Hence, the need for fewer fertilizers.

To give you additional information about this, the following is a session I did with nature in December 1990 on the nutrients and flower essence used in the Perelandra Soil Balancing Kit as well as whether folks should expand their kits, as I have done, to include a full set of essences and a wider range of soil nutrients and minerals.

COMBINED NATURE SESSION

Let us give you a working understanding of the soil balancers for Workbook II.

We understand that you have questioned whether the soil kit balancers need individual definitions similar to those given with the flower essences. They do not. Soil balancers do not work through healing patterns like flower essences do. The soil balancers address the molecular structure, strength and building needs of form or, in other words, the order and organization within form. They do this specifically on the molecular level.

There is no change in nitrogen, phosphorus and potash levels because soil balancing does not alter or add elements (solid matter) to a soil. The balancers are energetically applied within the molecular level specifically for the benefit of that level's structure, strength and building.

When the balancers are tested, each balancer offered is instantaneously fused with the form's molecular makeup to see which balancer or combination of balancers is needed to improve structure, strength and building. There is no definition-type patterning occurring here. We of nature will indicate which balancers do the best job within the molecular level.

The seven balancers in the Soil Balancing Kit were chosen by nature for the range of what they offer for strengthening and building the molecular structure of the soil form. Because of the overall environmental impact on the form being balanced, each balancer does not always interact the same way within the molecular level of the soil. Consequently, one cannot say that rock phosphate, for example, will always be needed for one specific, defined set of conditions because the impact of the environment surrounding the form changes the makeup and quality of the conditions within that form.

*Regarding the question about why kelp **and** liquid seaweed may be needed as balancers for the same form at the same time: Kelp and liquid seaweed (and other balancers that are similar to one another) may have similar properties but, from our perspective, they have a very different impact on form within the molecular level. It is the quality of impact that will differentiate between the two and tell us whether one or both are needed for the same form. It is not the similarity in their basic form properties but rather the quality of their impact upon the molecular level that determines what is needed.*

Comfrey was added to the Perelandra Soil Balancing Kit to serve as an "all-purpose" stabilizer. It is one flower essence that has within its properties the widest range of impact that covers the broadest range of needs within most form. If one is to expand his soil kit, we suggest that he first expand it with the flower essence stabilizers. The stabilizing part of the soil balancing/stabilizing process is what links that process to human intent, direction and purpose. When man balances and stabilizes form, he physically balances the nature elements, and then shifts the human intent, direction and purpose that have been fused with that form from one level to another. The use of a wide range of flower essences facilitates the stabilization process and enables the person doing the process to understand what is needed for stabilization to take place. It is in this area of the process that a person can discover patterning for learning purposes. Therefore, it is appropriate to have the benefit of the flower essence definitions.

Regarding the expansion of the basic soil balancing kit to include a wider range of soil amendments and minerals: We can work with the basic soil kit as it is offered at Perelandra. However, when we are given more balancers with which to work, we can assemble more complex and effective combinations of elements to impact the molecular level in a more sophisticated manner. From our point of view, it is strictly up to the person as to whether he will feel more comfortable working with the basic soil balancing kit during the process or using an expanded kit that includes more soil amendments and minerals.

We'd like to add another point: The name "Soil Balancing and Stabilizing Process" was given for this process because it was originally set up to balance and then stabilize soil. But any form can be balanced and stabilized using the same process, whether the form is soil or not. It can be "natural form" such as trees, rocks, land and sky. It can also be inanimate form such as machinery, furniture, equipment, tools . . . This process, therefore, is not limited to soil and, as we have seen with the Perelandra research, it can be used successfully to balance and stabilize any and all physical form because all physical form contains molecules. As we have said, the balancing and stabilizing process addresses the molecular level directly. It thus affects the form's order and organization, and also impacts the life vitality of that form. The result is that a new level of life vitality is reached that is in balance with the new level of order and organization.

Soil Balancing and Stabilizing Process Steps

To do this process, you will need your soil balancing kit (see appendix B) and the Perelandra Flower Essences (see appendix C for general information and ordering information).

1. Open a 4-point coning, if one is not already activated. *Add to it the Deva of Soil, if working with soil.* Verify your connection. Balance and stabilize the coning. Check yourself for essences.

2. State your intent to do the Soil Balancing and Stabilizing Process for a specific area. (Clearly describe the area, such as my garden, my full property, the south field, the woods, or physically be present at the site you wish to balance.)

3. Ask:
   What balancers are needed?
Then test all of the balancers included in your soil balancing kit. Whatever gets a positive response is what is needed for that section.

4. Now ask Pan to assist you. (Pan is already in the coning. You are simply focusing on Pan for this part of the process.)

5. Pour a small amount (about 1/8 teaspoon) of each balancer needed into a spoon or onto your hand. Hold the spoon or your hand out in front of you. State:
   I ask Pan to receive the energies from these balancers and shift them in the appropriate amounts and to the appropriate depth for the section we are working with.
Continue holding out your hand for about 10 seconds, giving ample time for the shift. Once completed, verify that the shift has occurred and drop the balancers on the ground. Don't try to save them because they are now form without energy and are no longer useful.

6. Turn your attention to the stabilizers—the flower essences. (If you do not have a set of flower essences, but you do have the Perelandra Soil Balancing Kit, you will be able to test for the need for Comfrey Essence, which is included in the kit for stabilization. It

is not as strong a stabilization as one gets when using the full sets of essences, but it is better than doing no stabilizing at all.) Ask:

What flower essences are needed for stabilization?

Test all of the essences you have available. Whatever tests positive is what is needed.

7. Place *1 drop* of each needed essence into your hand or a spoon and hold them out in front of you. State:

I ask Pan to receive the energies from these stabilizers and shift them in the appropriate amount and to the appropriate depth for the section we are working with.

Wait ten seconds for the shift to occur. Verify that the shift has occurred. Dry the essences from your hand or the spoon.

8. Spend a moment sensing the land or area you have just balanced and stabilized.

NOTE: You do not need to add the additional balancing and stabilizing steps to this process as you do to the other energy processes. The Soil Balancing and Stabilizing Process has its own balancing and stabilizing built in!

9. After thanking the team, close the coning by disconnecting from each member of the 4-point coning and the Deva of Soil.

10. Test yourself for flower essences. Take those that are needed and test for dosage.

NOTE: You can use the Soil Balancing and Stabilizing Process for larger, more general areas such as a field, meadow, garden, farm, woods, etc. And you can use this process to work with more precision in small areas such as a specific plant or row that seems to be in trouble, or for strengthening and balancing perennial plantings. In these cases, the soil being balanced and stabilized is that which is impacted by the specific plant or row. And, as nature has said, you can also use this process to balance and stabilize machines, equipment or other such objects. To work with the process, simply define what you intend to focus on and proceed through the Soil Balancing and Stabilizing Process for this smaller area or object exactly as you would for a larger area.

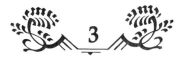

Atmospheric Balancing
Process

I first used this process in 1989 when nature showed me that, while the soil was being balanced nicely with the Soil Balancing and Stabilizing Process, it was equally important to address the atmosphere surrounding the garden. I saw the garden as a sandwich—the one piece of bread being the soil and the other piece of bread being the atmosphere. In between them were all the life forms comprising the middle part of the garden sandwich.

I also saw that the atmospheric space above the garden (or any defined land area) remains stationary while many different elements pass through it: birds, planes, radio waves, clouds, pollution . . . As a defined atmospheric space, it is as much in need of balancing and stabilizing as is the soil. Hence, the need for the Atmospheric Balancing Process.

After I sent this process to the Canadian soil scientist, he wrote: "The atmospheric balancing is really a beautiful process that seems to enhance the whole area. I am not sure of the connection, but since the atmospheric balancing, a severe drought has been broken in this area and the rainfall and weather have been just perfect. I definitely feel that the balancing contributed somewhat, since human stress in the atmosphere [can contribute to] imbalances such as droughts."

My own experience, after doing the atmospheric balancing, is that the area I am working with is now supported as much from above as it has been from below with soil balancing. I also have sensed a strong, clear, stabilizing link with the land to the universe, since the atmosphere being balanced extends from the land surface all the way up through the ozone layer to the larger universe.

For this process, use only the flower essences for both balancing and stabilizing. Do an atmospheric balancing under the same circumstances that require the soil balancing and stabilizing. I suggest that soil balancing and atmospheric balancing be treated as a unit and tested for together.

There is an exception that has to do with using the energy balancing and stabilizing processes on a new piece of land. I often find out, through testing, that I should first do the Soil Balancing and Stabilizing Process, along with other energy processes, and then the Atmospheric Balancing at some future date—several weeks or a couple of months down the road. Once I go through the first series of energy processes on new land, the healing and balancing of that land seem to strike a pattern where soil balancing and atmospheric balancing are then done in tandem.

NOTE: I get the information regarding which energy processes to use, in what order and when from the deva of the piece of land I am working with. In a coning, you are already connected with that deva. If, for example, you are working with a field or garden that is a part of a well-defined larger piece of land, you will need *both* the deva of the larger piece and the deva of the smaller piece in the coning. When I activate a coning, I begin with the Deva of Perelandra (the overlighting deva of the land I am working with as a whole) and then I include in the coning the Deva of the Garden. If I am working in the woods, I have the Deva of Perelandra and the Deva of the Perelandra Woods in my coning. If I then want to work in the meadow and I am finished with my work in the woods, I would request that I be disconnected from the Deva of the Perelandra Woods (verify my disconnection) and then ask to be connected with the Deva of the Meadow. Each section has its own pattern, timing and rhythm, and I can't assume that I get accurate information about the meadow from the Deva of the Woods.

It might be helpful to see a coning as a conference call in which you begin with your basic four members, and then add only those who are directly connected with the area and work you are presently doing. So if you have a 4-point coning with devas who are connected to a specific area, and then you want to switch your focus to another area, you need to disconnect from the devas involved in the first area and connect with the appropriate devas of the second area.

Devas are universal in dynamic, but some devas are regional by definition. I know that this may seem to be a contradiction, but the Deva of the Perelandra Meadow deals only with that meadow. By definition, the Perelandra meadow is limited to its boundaries. However, the Deva of Soil is global in its work. If I want to do the soil balancing for the meadow, I will have in my coning the devas of that meadow and of soil. If I then want to do a soil balancing for the garden, I will keep the Deva of Soil in the coning, disconnect from the deva of that meadow and connect with the Deva of the Garden.

There will be times when you are unsure who to link with. This is an easy corner to get out of. No matter what, open a 4-point coning, using as your devic connection the deva of the piece of land you are working with. After this, you can simply ask if other devas need to be included. Test, using kinesiology. If you get a positive and you can't figure out who it might be, simply request that the appropriate devas join your coning. The devas know who they are and will immediately link into the coning. To disconnect from these devas, ask that the appropriate devas who joined the coning for this work and who are unknown to you please disconnect from the coning now. The disconnection will occur immediately.

ATMOSPHERIC BALANCING PROCESS STEPS

Use flower essences for both balancing and stabilizing the atmosphere, but you will also need your soil balancing kit for a final soil balancing and stabilizing.

1. Picture/visualize the atmospheric area over the land you wish to balance. Extend that picture to 5 feet beyond the borders of the

land area. See a "column" forming straight up from the area (+ 5 feet) to just beyond the ozone layer at the beginning of outer space.

2. Open a 4-point coning and include the Deva of the Atmosphere. Verify the connections. Balance and stabilize the coning. Test yourself for any needed essences and take them.

3. Ask:

> What essences are needed for balancing the atmospheric space over this specific area of land? (Test essences.)

Place 1 drop of each essence into your hand or a spoon.

4. Ask Pan to assist you, and then state:

> I ask Pan to receive the energies from these essences and shift them appropriately to the atmosphere that is being *balanced.*

Hold out the essences for about 10 seconds. Verify that the shift has been made. Dry your hand or the spoon.

5. Ask:

> What essences are needed for stabilizing the atmospheric space over this specific area of land? (Test essences.)

Place 1 drop of each in your hand or a spoon.

6. State:

> I ask Pan to receive the energies from these essences and shift them appropriately to the atmospheric space that is being *stabilized.*

Hold out the solution for about 10 seconds. Verify that the shift has been made. Dry your hand or the spoon.

7. And now check to see if you need to balance and stabilize the land area itself. (Ask: "Does the land now need balancing and stabilizing?") Since the atmospheric balance has now changed, the land may need a comparable shift in its balance. Doing a regular balancing/stabilizing will facilitate this. Use the soil balancers for balancing and the flower essences for stabilizing.

8. This process is now completed and you may thank the team and close the coning. Verify that the coning is closed. Check yourself for essences and for needed dosage.

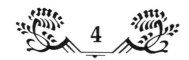

Geopathic Zones

Nature defines geopathic zones as being *"self-contained energy realities found within the planet's soil, water or air that can either enhance the health, balance and well-being of any life system that comes into contact with them or adversely impact, even destroy, some life systems that are impacted by them."* Geopathic zones are well-defined and detectable and can sometimes cause distress or illness to a person who lives or works in a zone-impacted area.

I first heard about geopathic zones in 1989 from Dr. Schatz. He had studied them and their effects for years. There is considerable information about their effects, primarily in the area of health. Researchers have found people living in the same area and having the same illness. Further research then showed that these people were all living on a geopathic zone. For example, some people with insomnia slept in beds located above geopathic zones.

To understand geopathic zones better, I asked nature for information in January 1990, in the following session with the 4-point coning plus the Deva of Soil and the Deva of Geopathic Zones.

NATURE SESSION

Geopathic zones are self-contained energy realities found within the planet's soil, water or air that can either enhance the health, balance and well-being of any life systems that come into contact with them or adversely impact, even destroy, some life systems that are impacted by them. In recent years, humans have become more aware of geopathic zones because of the detrimental impact these zones have had on those living within a zone area. The impact may range from mild discomfort, sleep difficulties and constant but mild illnesses to chronic, life-threatening conditions.

But geopathic zones are complex and cannot be adequately covered in one short definition. Therefore, they should not be looked at solely as mysterious life-threatening forces. What have been referred to as "geopathic zones" do not always originate from the same circumstances nor do they function with the same dynamics. Geopathic zones can refer to a soil/earth phenomenon, a rock-vein phenomenon, a waterway phenomenon and an atmospheric phenomenon. They may consist of any one of these or include a combination of several in order to create a larger, more complex geopathic zone.

In order to understand how geopathic zones form, one must look at them from two separate perspectives: the human perspective and the nature perspective. Let us address the nature perspective first. If one were to view the planet without human habitation, one would see a nature-dominant planet in which cycles, rhythms, patterns and movement play out in an unrestricted, natural way. In this environment, elements of the planet—the elements comprising the soil and its core, those elements that are a part of the planet's surface, and the elements comprising the atmosphere—would shift and move as part of the planet's natural patterns. We point this out to you to emphasize that one cannot say that geopathic zones are created solely by humans and are caused by adverse human impact on the planet. This is not true. Left on its own, the natural rhythm of the planet would include a natural movement and shifting of its elements in such a way as to create a physical environment that humans call "geopathic zones."

These zones may be seen as veins, as broad areas, as circles and as wide swaths narrowing into thinner swaths. They may occur above ground, on the surface and below ground. Their depth varies as much as their width. From the broadest perspective, they are a concentration of "like" matter. We refer you back to the principle of horizontal compatibility—like attracting like—for it is the natural magnetic phenomenon of horizontal compatibility occurring between elements on all levels that creates the kinds of zones of which we now speak. As the earth's elements shift and move, you will find that the key to understanding this movement is horizontal compatibility: like moving into the direction and vicinity of like.

The result is the creation of compatible environments. (You keep seeing a field of wildflowers. This picture is from us.) Using that field of wildflowers as an example, we of nature would say that this is a perfect visual example of horizontal compatibility. Now, many humans would look at such a field and say that the wildflowers that grow there do so because the physical conditions are correct for supporting their growth. And that the wildflowers that do not grow in the field are absent because the physical conditions do not support their growth. We of nature look at the field and say it is a compatible environment created by the natural magnetic attraction of horizontally compatible elements, including those wildflowers. It is, as an environment, excluding nothing. From our point of view, this is a geopathic zone and can be defined in size and scope by the compatible elements growing in the zone and supported by that zone.

We use the imagery of the wildflower field purposely. Many feel that geopathic zones are, by definition, "negative." Often this is because geopathic zones can be powerful in terms of an energy dynamic—the sum being greater and more powerful than its parts. Also, these zones can feel exceptionally powerful to humans because the parts or elements in a specific zone may be, in and of themselves, especially powerful. Some zones create and emit an energy that can be described as gentle, some soft, others strong, and still others powerful beyond that which some humans can endure.

Now, add humans to the planet. If given total freedom, humans would automatically shift and move around the planet in response to the natural earth shifts that are occurring. The human soul and body would seek a compatible environment. We include the human soul because the body, although comprised of nature, is shaped and molded by the individual's soul. Consequently, humans would seek horizontal compatibility as a unit.

Let us, at this point, address the geopathic zones that adversely impact and cause problems to humans. Like attracts like. That which the human creates and releases on the planet adds to and becomes a part of that which defines the planet. Nothing magically disappears. Another way of saying this is that nothing dies. That which is in mass form becomes a part of the environment on which it sits. Feelings and emotions have a more ebb-and-

flow dynamic to them. Several things can occur with feelings and emotions. One is that, once emitted, they will become a part of the environment in which they were emitted. If the emotions were expressed and resolved in a complete and balanced manner, they will become a part of that environment as an element already in balance. If the emotions were not "grounded" and therefore not resolved, they will become a part of that environment as an unbalanced element. If allowed to remain as part of the environment, as has been the case with most emotional input throughout the planet, those emotions will impact everything else that is part of that environment and initiate a movement of accommodation of the environmental elements towards the unbalanced emotion. In short, the molecules comprising the environment in which the ungrounded emotions are impacting will change. And because of horizontal compatibility, any elements that were part of a heretofore balanced environment that cannot make the molecular changes required to enfold the new unbalanced emotional element will move out of that environment, first in energy and then followed by form, to a more compatible environment.

As the molecules within an environment alter to accommodate the emotional input, that environment attracts to it a different range of elements. There is a new horizontal compatibility. This is what you refer to as an "emotional sinkhole." The new environment will also naturally attract to it humans who are comfortable with the range and quality of emotions supported by it. Often, once imbalance becomes integrated into an environment, it encourages even greater imbalance. This may appear to contradict "like attracting like" or horizontal compatibility. But one of the dynamics of imbalance is that it encourages an intensification of the problem. Conversely, one of the dynamics of balance is that it encourages an intensification of balance as well as the corresponding movement forward to a new level of balance. So, in terms of the environment that is now not in balance, you have a downspiraling effect that was initiated by humans through the release of unbalanced emotional energy. The initial imbalance as well as the downspiraling are both initiated by humans. Nature does not have as part of its makeup the mechanism that would create and initiate an emotional downspiral.

Let us give you an example of geopathic zones. We will address a small urban row house that is sitting on one larger geopathic zone that has as part of its makeup several intersecting line-like zones. These are several "environments" that are complete within themselves and are related to one another in terms of compatibility. The occupants have detected two line-like zones by using dowsing techniques. But, there are in actuality five more intersecting line-like zones moving through their property and house. You will find that in heavily populated areas, where humans and nature have had high impact, the complexity of geopathic zones will increase.

Now what is occurring in this home is an example of how humans, using free will and strength in determination, can stop an environmental geopathic downspiral. These occupants are not people who have naturally gravitated to an environment in which they are completely comfortable. They have exercised free will and taken on an environment that, in some ways (and not all), is uncomfortable and they have moved to change it. This same phenomenon occurs in urban areas that are going through renovation and renewal. New people deliberately choose to move in with the intent to revitalize and change an area. In our example, the two line-like zones that were detected are the two zones that are most out of balance with the occupants. They detected the zones because of an especially strong electrical charge that is being set up due to difference; that is, the people living there are so different in makeup from the two line zones that an especially charged electrical field has developed between them and the zones, making detection not only possible but essential. For the health and well-being of the occupants, the geopathic zones must be addressed.

*Regarding the process to use when working with the geopathic zones: The intent is to return the zone(s) to a strong environmental **balance**. Automatically, those elements in the zone that do not reflect the new balance will be released to continue on an evolutionary path (as in the case of emotional energy) or will shift to another more compatible zone (as in the case of nature and mass). Returning the zones to balance is easily accomplished with the Energy Cleansing Process and Battle Energy Release. We recommend that the Energy Cleansing Process be done prior to the Battle Energy Release so that non-related emotional energy can be appropriately released, thus preparing the area for the Battle Energy Release. In the case of working with geopathic zone balance, you will more often than not be addressing nature after it has shifted molecularly to accommodate the imbalance. In short, these are old problems. Consequently, you will have to do a soil balancing followed by a soil stabilization to assist the shift and stability of the molecular makeup of the nature involved.*

For geopathic zone balancing, we suggest that you start the Energy Cleansing and Battle Energy Release Processes at a depth of 25 feet below the lowest point in the house or land, i.e., the 25 feet below the floor of a basement or land valley. This will assure that all the various depths of the geopathic zone involved will be included. The majority of geopathic zone work will automatically be taken care of when a person does the Energy Cleansing, Battle Energy Release and Soil Balancing and Stabilizing Processes. We would estimate that 3/4 of these "problem" zones are within the 5-foot surface level or, in the case of working with a home with a basement, 5 feet below the bottom-most floor of the house. However, a depth of 25 feet will cover all necessary zones and situations without exception.

NOTE: If you will recall, the energy process work extends to a height of 5 feet above the highest point. The geopathic zones that are contained in this area will also be taken care of automatically with the three energy processes. Rarely do the ones that can cause problems for humans extend above this height. However, for those rare few that extend beyond, the Atmospheric Balancing and Stabilizing Process will restore their balance. One may discover if the geopathic zones they wish to balance extend above the highest-point-plus-5-feet range by asking the Deva of Geopathic Zones:

Do the zones we are balancing extend above the highest-point-plus-5-feet range?

If yes, do the Atmospheric Balancing Process, using flower essences, once you have completed the soil balancing and stabilizing.

The process: Open a 4-point coning and include the Deva of Geopathic Zones, the Deva of Soil and, if not already included, the deva of the property through which the zone in question runs. You'll be working with Pan for this kind of work. Shift the coning appropriately as you move through the Energy Cleansing Process, the Battle Energy Release Process and the Soil Balancing and Stabilizing Process.

GEOPATHIC ZONE BALANCING PROCESS STEPS

Have your flower essences and soil balancing kit ready.

1. Open a 4-point coning + the Deva of Geopathic Zones, the Deva of Soil and the deva of the land area or property through which the zone runs, if not already included.

Balance and stabilize the coning. Test yourself for essences and take any that you need.

2. Do the Energy Cleansing Process.

You do not need to open a coning (step 4) specially for this process since a coning has already been activated. However, include the balancing and stabilizing step (step 16) before moving on. You will be balancing and stabilizing as a unit the zones and the overall land area that you have just impacted when you did this process.

3. Do the Battle Energy Release Process.

Include the balancing and stabilizing step again (step 6) to support the zones/land that has been impacted by this process.

4. Do the Soil Balancing and Stabilizing Process.

You do not need to balance and stabilize the balancing and stabilizing process!

5. The Geopathic Zone Balancing Process is complete. Thank the team and close the coning. Check yourself for essences and a dosage. Pat yourself on the back.

Dr. Schatz and I have used this process a number of times on geopathic zones. He verified the presence of the zone through dowsing, did the process and then waited the devically specified time for the process to complete the zone shift. Then he did a sequential time test using kinesiology to discover when to retest the zones for verification. The zones needed anywhere from 2 to 5-1/2 hours. He then returned to the area and, using L-rods, checked the zone. Each time, the zone was completely neutralized and no longer detectable.

NOTE: The positions of geopathic zones do not need to be located. Nature knows where they are. Just find out if any zones are present in a defined land area and in need of neutralizing.

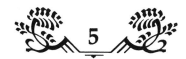

Plant Triangulation

In the fall of 1989, I found out from nature a rather odd but interesting thing. Plants growing in a garden are linked in groups of three to create strong, balanced, interrelated triangle units. The points of the triangle are three different plants or plant varieties—for example, parsley, green beans and sage. These three points have among them connecting links of energy. In a fully balanced and stabilized triangle, the points and the links are strong. I called a meeting with nature to find out more about this triangulation business.

GARDEN SESSION
9 September 1989
Garden Coning: 4-point coning + Deva of the Perelandra Garden

Machaelle: At this time, I would like to get information concerning the triangles that are created in the garden. What are they, how were they formed and why, how do they work, what relationship, if any, do they have with one another—and do I have the complete process for working with them with you?

Coning: The triangles that are a part of a co-creative garden are really nothing new within the natural scheme of things. The triangle concept is based on what you would call "interplanting" and is but an extension of

PLANT
TRIANGULATION

the simple plant-next-to-plant concept with which most organic gardeners are familiar.

We are referring to two separate kinds of interplanting, the first being the plant-next-to-plant. This involves two or more plants growing next to one another for the purpose of mutual strengthening and balance. As you know, this is the most readily understood concept of interplanting.

The second kind concerns itself with a specific, defined area of environment and relates to the linking of individual components within that environment. A garden is a specific, defined area of environment. Within vast areas of open land, the defined space may be the entire area or it may be a number of smaller defined spaces that together comprise the larger area. We of nature, of course, are quite aware of the location of these areas. Often they are discernible to the human eye. One large area of open land may include a forest, a wood's edge, a swamp area . . . Each one of these areas can be defined as a specific environment within itself. Together they create one interrelated whole. But we would like to focus on the interrelationships occurring within each separate area, for this is where the triangulation that you were introduced to in the Perelandra garden takes place.

We in nature are always concerned with strength and balance. Much of the strength and balance within a natural setting takes place on what humans would refer to as an energy level. That is, the elements of strength and balance within the makeup of a specific area are occurring in unseen ways on unseen levels. To us, the strength and balance of energy is primary to that of form, and is the key to strength and balance in form. As you have discovered in the co-creative garden, what goes into the garden and its placement relates to energy. The strong and balanced qualities of the form in the garden are the natural results of its energy. Consequently, when we work to create a garden environment with a human gardener, we build into the plan a number of considerations that, on an energy level, serve to strengthen and balance the individual components and the whole.

Triangulation is one of these built-in considerations. We not only do work to establish strength and balance between two plants growing side by side, but we also will appropriately link each variety of plant to two other varieties growing within the same defined environment. This creates a triangle among these three points or three plant varieties. The triangle creates a linked, three-point configuration of especially heightened energy that serves to balance and strengthen each point of the triangle a thousand fold beyond that which would have been accomplished had no triangulation taken place and had the gardener depended solely on the plant-next-to-plant interplanting.

Triangulation does not occur unless all three points of a triangle are "properly" placed, both with respect to themselves and within the larger whole. These triangles are not random. Their specific sizes, angles and points all play a part in the creation of the triangles. Don't lose sight of the fact that we establish a triangular vortex of energy for the purpose of creating strength and balance in all that comprises the triangle. We are not interested in creating a blast furnace of energy, nor do we bother creating a triangle when little, if any, energy would result.

In the garden that is created solely from the human mind, virtually no triangles exist. We say "virtually" because from time to time the human mind has actually placed the proper plants in the correct alignment, which activated a triangle. We consider this a fluke. From the rare occurrences we've observed, we would have to say that the creation of triangles within a garden or landscaping project is not something the human mind naturally grasps at this time. Conversely, in a co-created garden in which nature is allowed to design and plan from the devic level, triangles are automatically included as a part of that design.

The components of the triangle that are of importance when talking about strength and balance are the three points and the connecting energy lines that link the three points. When a soil balancing is done for a specific variety of plant, it raises the vitality level between the plant and its soil, thus strengthening and balancing that one point of the triangle. Once this is done for all three varieties of plants that comprise a single triangle, you have solid, stable, balanced points. This is when the three points connect via an "energy shaft"—and now you have a triangle. The degree of balance and strength among the three points relates directly to the balance and strength of the connecting energy lines.

These lines or shafts are as much of a reality as the three visible points. They run straight through the form that might exist in their path, and they do not alter or hinder that form. This is because the lines are part of a triangular formation with strong relationship to the three points only. They do not disperse, alter or weaken because of any other points or elements of form that might be in their path. We might add here that not every aspect of form within a given area is triangulated. Some form exists alone in *strength and balance in certain situations, while other forms relate solely to the plant-next-to-plant interplanting and do not need to be triangulated for strength and balance beyond this interplanting relationship. All of these things are considered when a devic plan is conceived.*

You have experienced weakness in this year's garden due to weaknesses that developed in the triangle lines or links, not in the points. Consequently, when a soil balancing was done for the purpose of shoring up the plants in question, only the point was affected. The connecting lines are realities within themselves and must be addressed separately.

When there is a weakness—something that might occur from a sudden shift in the prevailing ecological picture—it is important to focus not simply on the single weak point in the garden. You must also identify the other two varieties to which this weak point relates in the triangle. This can be done by connecting with the deva of the garden or the nature spirit level working with the weakened plants. Once the other two points are identified, you will have the triangle with which to work. First eliminate a point problem by testing to see if a soil balance, essence foliar feeding or nutritional change is needed for any of the points. Don't assume the weak-looking point, the point that originally caught your attention, is the crux of the problem. It might well be one of the other points, or both, or all three. Energy from the first point could well be drained off to another point during the crucial stage of growth, leaving the first point appearing weakened and the second appearing healthy.

Once the three points are attended to, check to see if the connecting energy lines of the triangle are open, strong and functioning properly. A shift in a point can alter the operational ability of the connecting lines. Approach this as you would an atmospheric balancing process. Only now, instead of focusing on the atmosphere over a given area, focus on a specific energy line that links two points within a triangle. Work with the three lines separately, not collectively. For this process, you will need to use flower essences only.

The triangles in a garden environment form automatically in the spring, once all of the points of a specific triangle are introduced into the garden and balanced. The components of all of the triangles can be given to you once you have drawn the large garden chart. However, if at planting time there is a change in placement or variety, the corresponding triangle will have to be re-identified. Again, because of changes in the environment, there may be a shift that could affect several triangles. Therefore, to ward off confusion, we advise you to identify the triangles either once the garden is fully planted or at the time when a weakened area crops up. (Pardon the pun.) Quite frankly, this is a new area of partnership between nature and humans. The results of what we suggest you do now will enable us to plan next year's garden more effectively.

We do have one other suggestion: If all the triangles are identified after the garden planting is completed, it would be good to connect with each triangle and test its three points and three lines for proper balance and strength. We see this being done for the Perelandra garden around the first two weeks of June. And as you move through the phase 3 weekly meetings [the weekly garden meetings I have with the nature intelligences during the period beginning in mid-June through early October], it would be good to test each triangle for strengthening and balancing needs. For this, you do not have to identify each point and line of every triangle for testing. You have a total of twenty triangles this year. Identifying each by focusing on one plant variety that constitutes one of its points is enough. In short, you can say, "Does the cauliflower triangle need balancing or strengthening?" If yes, then be sure to work with all three points and lines comprising that triangle.

A point regarding work with farms: There is a triangular relationship that exists among fields that is much the same as the relationship that exists among plants in a garden. The points need to be identified and the lines kept strong and balanced. Each year, as the field crops and field uses rotate, the triangles will change. Overall farm balance will be greatly assisted if these larger triangles are identified and maintained.

Machaelle: If a succession planting is done in a garden, is a new triangle formed and an old one dismantled, or what?

Coning: If the succession planting is done from the devic plan—that is, if it is a part of the original plan and is placed devically—it will automatically slip into the existing triangle that was established earlier with the first planting.

We read your next question: Where something has been planted that has an early growth and maturity cycle (such as lettuce or peas) yet is not present during the mid-season cycle, the triangle is still operating. That one point is fully "grounded" into the garden and, even though the plant is no longer physically present, its presence is still there. Early plantings remain very much a part of the full garden cycle whether they are present in visible form or not. A succession planting operates in an early planting position very much as it would in a normal plant-next-to-plant interplanting. This is why it is important to plant a succession planting according to the devic plans. In a triangle situation, the second planting forms with the energy of the first planting and establishes itself in the point of the triangle in perfect balance.

Machaelle: Once the points and triangles are established in a garden season, are they likely to change or shift?

Coning: No. Their balance and strength may change, but the triangles established during planting will remain throughout the season. This, of course, hinges on the gardener planting according to the original devic plan. A plan will not include the dismantling of a triangle in a season. If the gardener unwittingly removes one of the points out of timing, the triangle will first be drastically weakened. If that missing point is not shored up fairly quickly (the plants replaced or new seed planted), the triangle will dismantle and the energy will disperse. Also, you will see an effect on the other two points.

Machaelle: You said yesterday, while I was working with this in the garden, that the weakness of one triangle will not weaken the other triangles. Did I get that right?

Coning: Yes. Each triangle is a self-contained unit of energy. It does not drain off nor does it distort the strength and balance of the other triangles. In the overall picture, however, a weakened triangle will not enhance the balance, strength or stability of the full, defined area. In this way, it will affect the whole.

Machaelle: I don't have any more questions now. I think I'll close. Even though it is late in the season, I will institute a triangle check in next week's garden session.

Coning: Good. We look forward to this. By the way, as you have guessed, the random-looking flower essence foliar feeding that occurred in the garden this summer often related to the balance and strengthening of the points of the triangles.

Machaelle: You're right. That's what I figured. I'm going to shift the coning now. Thank you.

Coning: You're most welcome. Thank you! (Close coning.)

I felt I needed more information about this triangulation business, so I followed up that session with another one in early spring.

GARDEN SESSION
Garden Coning—10 March 1990

Coning: Good afternoon. We are aware of the questions you have about the garden triangles and, if you wish, we can begin by addressing these questions.

Machaelle: Yes. Go ahead.

*Coning: We will address the patterning of the triangles in the garden. Of course you already understand, or shall we say "suspect," that the triangle patterns relate to more that just the three plants or points involved in each triangle. When we triangulate within nature, it is in response to the immediate environment in which the triangle is situated, as well as the relationship of that immediate environment to the larger whole. One cannot isolate a defined nature environment from the rest of the global environment and universal environment any more than one can isolate a human from these things. The purpose of the triangles is to establish strength and balance in relationship to the immediate environment **and** the larger environments. In turn, the triangles impact both the immediate and larger environments by introducing into them an especially heightened and strengthened energy. It is important to see that the triangles both affect the relatively small area in which they sit, shoring up these smaller areas where the surrounding ecology is unbalanced and damaged, and impact the whole by introducing into it an especially strong and balanced triangle of energy.*

*Triangles "serve" the points and connecting links of that which goes into the makeup of the triangles, **and** triangles "serve" the whole. If you are to understand why we of nature are most anxious to introduce the concept of triangulation to humans, you must see both the immediate and the extended impact of triangles.*

When Earth was "nature-dominant," we of nature assured a strong networking of triangles around the surface of the planet. This created a special nature leyline grid consisting of a vibration of harmonious energy around the planet as well as emanating from the planet. Now that the planet is "human-dominant," it is nearly impossible for us to assure more than a relatively few triangles within nature. Humans have impacted this level of what can be referred to as "energy ecology" as much as they have impacted the more physical levels of ecology. In order to restore the planet to its potential level of resonant balanced energy, we must work with you to establish new triangles in a new form of triangle networking throughout the planet. The co-creative gardening system is an excellent means for establishing these triangles. Because we are an active part of this system, we can plan for and introduce triangles within the context of a garden. At this point in time, the full ramifications as to why a triangle would be established cannot be perceived by humans, and you will have to rely on our input for proper placement and interrelationship among the triangles.

We might add here that a total of 24 triangles established within a 100-feet-in-diameter garden area is high in number, and they are most complex in their interrelationship. We do not see such a large number of triangles being established in the family-oriented co-creative garden. An average family garden count would be 8 to 10 triangles. The large number in the Perelandra garden relates to the intent of the garden (it is a research and teaching garden) and the fact that the balance is now such that it can hold and sustain such a complex triangulation. At this point in time, we have taken the opportunity to establish this complex triangulation at Perelandra because what resonates out from the Perelandra garden serves to stabilize the planetary whole at a time when global ecology is shaky and weak. In relating to others the principle and process of triangulation, you will need to have this information so that you can shift their focus from the intensity of the Perelandra garden to a more manageable triangulation that will occur in their family-oriented gardens and farms.

Machaelle: I need to ask a couple of technical questions. I have four "points" in the garden that serve as "double points" and are a part of two different triangles. I'm assuming that this is correct identification on my part.

Coning: Yes—and now you wish to know how to work with these double points. You have already received insight that we have given you about these double points. We will verify what you have received.

*The two triangles that share one point do indeed relate as triangles to one another. If you find that the shared point needs balancing, you will need to check the balance of the points and links of **both** triangles. If another point in one of the triangles needs balancing—here we refer to the* *points other than the double points—you will not have to concern yourself with checking the second triangle that is connected by the double point for possible strengthening. The second triangle will only be affected if the shared or double point is in need of balancing. Regarding this issue, you need only concern yourself with the six points of a double-pointed triangle and not with the connecting energy links among the points. A connecting link is not shared between two triangles—they share only a double point.*

Machaelle: What about the vegetables, flowers and herbs that are not a part of any triangles?

Coning: These are not "weak spots" in the garden. Only a certain number of triangles within any environment, be it garden or wild, is appropriate. Therefore, within any environment there are usually many places/plants that are not linked into a triangle. The plants that are "outside" the triangle system in your garden are perfectly capable of "standing" on their own in a fully balanced way.

Machaelle: Do you want me to do balancing work on these triangles while they are out of form, i.e., before the garden is planted? This would be a change from the process that was indicated in the fall when we first talked about triangulation. At that time, you suggested that the garden be completely planted prior to identifying and working with triangles. Now I sense a change in this procedure.

Coning: Yes, you can go ahead and do the initial balancing and stabilizing on the triangles prior to planting, and this is a change. The improvements in the Workbook's environment-process chart procedure this season have allowed us to alter our approach to the triangle work. The chart work was greatly facilitated by the introduction of the double-check/verification timing.

[After each *Workbook* chart process was completed, while I was still in the simplified-chart stage, I waited for 48 hours, at nature's request, and then checked the information with nature to verify that it was still accurate. Nature used the 48 hours to place that information into effect in the garden, on the energy level, and to observe its impact on the garden and the garden environment. When I opened the coning after the 48 hours I would often find that some changes had been made. I would then indicate the changes on the chart, wait another 48 hours, open the coning and check the information again. I checked all the information that I had gotten in that specific process, not just what had been changed. I would continue doing this until everything "held."

Then I would go on to the next chart or environmental process and add this new information to the mix, allowing for the 48-hour check along the way. When I finished with the environmental processes, I did one final check on all of the information: planting position, ratio, color, interplanting, etc. This would assure that all the information had "held." By the time I actually planted the garden, the various elements were in place on the energy level, had been checked, modified and verified, and nature and I were confident that we had the strongest layout that this garden could handle.

Prior to this modification in the *Workbook* environmental processes, we co-creative gardeners would experience a bit of juggling around in the garden once it was planted. For example, out of five green pepper plants, one might die for no apparent reason. But nature saw that a slight change in the green pepper ratio would strengthen the overall garden. They had said to me that, if there was a question about ratio or about any of the other environmental information, they would allow for that question in their information and give us the maximum number or amount for planning purposes—and then adjust the plants accordingly once they were planted. With the 48-hour check, all that kind of modification is done on the energy level and changed on the charts.]

Coning continued: The triangles, though not visible to the human eye, are already in place and functioning just as the garden plan is already in place and functioning. The planting process that you go through from this point on is but a physical mirror of that which already exists, and it provides physical vessels into which this energy can completely ground. So, one need not wait for this grounding in order to work with and affect that which already exists in energy.

We suggest that you first do the overall Perelandra/garden soil balancing and stabilizing work that is scheduled for next Friday before you do any triangle balancing. The former will support and stabilize the latter. Work from the new triangle identification chart and test for points of weakness as you did in the garden last fall. If a connecting link is weak and none of the triangle's points are weakened, we will still indicate a problem

Making a triangle identification chart is explained on page 71.

in that triangle when you test one of the triangle points. Then, all you will need to do for proper link balancing and stabilizing is identify if it is the link between points 1 and 2, 2 and 3, or 3 and 1 that is weak. We believe this will facilitate your testing.

Machaelle: Yes, it will. Are you setting this up as a general rule for everyone who will be working with triangulation, or does each person need to set up a testing system with you for himself?

Coning: We will make this a general rule. See the testing of the triangle points as entry to the entire triangle system. Once a point tests weak, the specific weakened point(s) and/or link(s) will need to be identified through testing. If a point tests positive and strong, one can assume this to mean that all points and links within that specific triangle are strong and balanced.

Machaelle: Is the ratio information going to change once the triangle balancing is done on an energy level?

Coning: No. The ratio and color patterning were designed with balanced triangulation in mind.

Machaelle: Do I need to get further timing for doing the first triangle work beyond "after the Perelandra/garden soil balancing work"?

*Coning: No. Anytime **soon** after the soil balancing will be fine. It would be easier for you to do the triangle work on the energy level prior to planting. This is why we say "soon."*

Machaelle: I'm going to have to heel-in onion plants and strawberry plants in R/A 7. Will this affect the triangle work at all?

Coning: No. We understand your intent to be of a temporary nature when heeling-in plants. Consequently, that temporary soil use does not affect the garden plan or energy balance work. It will, however, affect the soil fertilizer needs of that specific row for the plants that are planned for this area. We take this into consideration when we give you the soil fertilizer needs for the row.

Machaelle: I'm almost afraid to ask this question, but it *does* beg to be asked. Is there further triangulation going on in the garden area among the perennials? This would include the wildflower areas, meadow, grass, perennial ring, roses, etc.

Coning: Yes, of course. But you need not concern yourself with these triangles. As you point out, they are comprised of perennial plants, trees and bushes, and have long since been balanced because of the fertilizer and soil balancing work you have done in these areas. The soil balancing you did for the individual rose bushes last season related in part to the triangle question. That individual bush balancing need not be done this year. In fact, you do not need to do individual soil balancing for the entire perennial ring this year. A triangle comprised of perennials will hold its balance and strength quite well once balance and strength are obtained. In short, all of the perennial triangles in the Perelandra garden area are balanced and holding well. You may see these triangles as a larger networking into which fit the smaller, more intricate garden triangles made up of the annuals. If you wish, we will be most happy to work with you to identify this larger triangle system at any time.

Machaelle: Thank you. I'll do that sometime in the next few months so that I can see what it looks like. I'm pleased to know that I won't have to do all that individual perennial soil balancing this year. Should I check with you each year regarding this issue of individual balancing and stabilizing of perennials to see if additional work needs to be done?

Coning: Yes. Make it a part of your fertilizing and planting rhythm questions for late winter/early spring. Additional work will rarely be needed. This is due, in part, to the overall quality of the Perelandra nature balance. It is much easier for these perennial triangles, both in the garden area and throughout Perelandra as a whole, to maintain strength and balance because of the quality of the co-creative work. When explaining this part of triangulation to others, we suggest that you simply tell them to check annually regarding perennial triangulation.

Machaelle: Were both the points and the connecting links balanced last year? I didn't work with the connecting links when I did the individual balancing of the perennials.

Coning: That work has been accomplished through the overall soil balancing and atmospheric balancing. The triangles established within a garden that is primarily comprised of annuals have a finite "life span" that is limited to one growing season. This makes it necessary to address the balance questions quickly in order for those triangles to function well. This is one reason why we have waited until now to introduce garden triangulation. They must be co-created between humans and nature as well as maintained quickly by both humans and nature. With perennial triangles, balance can be achieved gradually and over a longer period of time. But, as we pointed out earlier, the number of perennial triangles around the planet has been reduced to a relative handful due to the impact of human population upon the planet.

We will give you an example to use when talking to others about triangulation and its importance. When a person asks us whether a specific tree or bush should be removed from their land, we automatically take into consideration the issue of that tree or bush being a part of a perennial triangle. If it is, and this triangle is especially important to the overall health and balance of the land, we will say "no." To remove one point of the triangle will dismantle the entire triangle. In the case of especially old trees or bushes (or boulders, we might add), we are even more reluctant to give the go-ahead for removal because the age of the tree, for example, is an indication that the triangle is especially well-established and strong. An equally strong and balanced triangle cannot be instantaneously created for "replacement" of the one that is being dismantled.

Machaelle: I take it that when a person works with you in a co-creative manner to establish landscaping with perennials, triangle creation is taken into consideration in much the same manner as when we work with you to create an annual vegetable garden.

Coning: That is correct. Triangulation is something that is automatically considered when we work with you and give details of the devic plan. Triangulation within any land/environmental area is automatically included.

Machaelle: Would you recommend that a landscaper identify the perennial triangles and do balance work as part of the job?

Coning: Yes. But we must say that, at this point, just getting landscapers to shift from control landscaping to co-creative landscaping would be a vital first step. The various energy balances, soil balance processes, fertilizer processes and triangle balancing would become important parts of the work once they have made the shift to a co-creative focus.

At this time, we would like to address a question someone has asked you about triangulation and coning, and which is best to use during interlevel work or communication. Triangulation can be set up for these purposes, but because of the nature of a coning and how it differs from the nature of triangulation, we recommend that the coning be used.

The coning creates a vortex of energy that serves to stabilize and facilitate the different participants in an interlevel communication. It can be easily activated and dismantled and, therefore, is easy to use for a relatively short period of time. Also, a coning can accommodate more participants than a triangle. For example: For you to work with a specific garden question in which more than a simple yes/no is required, you would need yourself, the deva of the plant concerned and a nature spirit representative. This would imply a triangle. But this "mix" does not have good balance as a coning—it does not have involution/evolution balance.

To achieve that, you need to include a connection to the White Brotherhood dynamic to insure that all elements are represented and are in a balanced coning mix. You now have 4 points—1 point beyond a triangle. If you are only asking quick yes/no information such as when one is working with the environmental processes, only 2 points need to be activated: you and either a nature spirit or a deva. The processes in the Workbook were set up to include the human and a deva or a nature spirit because this eliminates any problems a human new to the co-creative environment processes might have in discerning what nature intelligence level to activate for which questions. It was not meant to imply a triangle.

We recommend, because of the dynamics involved in interlevel work, whether it is between human souls from different levels or humans and nature intelligences, that the coning be set up and used.

Machaelle: One thing that comes to my mind is that a coning is something that doesn't just form. It must be specifically called together and activated. One doesn't look around and suddenly find a coning in existence. It's an extremely controlled situation.

Coning: That is correct, and this is one reason why it is better to utilize a coning for doing interlevel work than to attempt to link a triangle. The two have very different dynamics, and the coning dynamic fits the interlevel-information function much better than does the triangle dynamic. Conversely, attempting to create conings as a connecting, balancing and strengthening network throughout the garden would be most inappropriate. It would seem a disaster. In essence, you would be using a hammer to do the job best suited for a saw.

Machaelle: Right now, I have no further questions or thoughts—on anything! I think I'll close the coning and go read my latest trash novel.

*Coning: For you we will agree that this is a fine idea. You know how to
find us!*

Machaelle: Thank you. (Close coning.)

PLANT TRIANGULATION PROCESS STEPS

Making the Triangle Identification Chart

1. Make a second garden chart with the location of all the
vegetable, herb and flower areas and rows in the garden. You do
not need to indicate ratio or color—just plant location.

2. Identify the triangles in your garden:

a) Test each plant *variety* (not individual plants of the same
variety) to find out if it is a triangle point.

b) With each triangle point, test the other plant varieties in the
garden to discern which ones form the other two points of the triangle. If your garden is in sections, you can make this process more
efficient by testing to see what section(s) the other two points are in,
thus eliminating the need to test unnecessary areas. Or you can test
your garden row by row to locate the rows the other two points are
in, and then test the plant varieties in the row to identify the point
location. Once a triangle point is located, mark the spot on the chart
with a dot. When you have marked the three points that belong to
one triangle you are working to identify, simply connect the dots—
and you have an identified triangle. Do this for all of the varieties
that test as a point.

HINT: You may find, for example, that a 25-foot row of green
beans is a "point." The 25-foot area functions as a single triangle
point, even though visually we see it as a 25-foot-long line or row.
Place a dot on your chart anywhere along the row.

AN ADDITIONAL HINT: It is helpful if you color code each triangle
with its own color. As you work with the triangle chart throughout
the summer, it is tedious to locate the points and links of a specific
triangle if all the dots and lines are in one color. Giving each set of
triangle dots and lines its own color cleans up this problem.

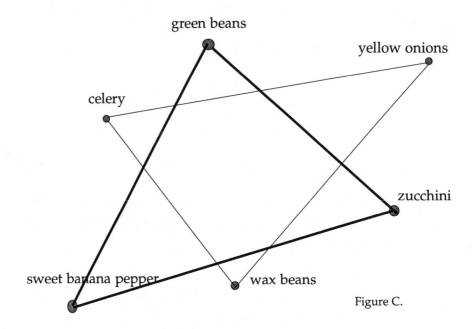

Figure C.

NOTE: A perennial plant can be triangulated with other perennials such as a tree or bush and it can have objects such as a large rock as a point. It can also be triangulated with a larger area such as a woodsedge or meadow. In this case, the entire space is the point, but for convenience, you may draw a small dot anywhere within the larger space. This will give you something to connect your linking line to.

*Also, if you have a triangle that tests for a weak point or link yet, when you test for the specific balancers you come up with nothing, test to see if, in this case, the balancers **and** the stabilizers are the flower essences. You'll test the essences twice. This won't come up often and, when it does, it usually will occur when you are working with a link within a perennial triangle. But, it can also occur with an annual triangle. In this instance, you will test the essences twice, as well.*

Many of the triangles will overlay one another like the two triangles above.

You now have your triangle identification chart.

Triangle Balancing Process Steps

Have your triangle identification chart, soil balancing kit and flower essences ready.

1. Open a 4-point coning and include the deva of your garden, if it is not already included. Balance and stabilize the coning. Test yourself for essences.

2. Using your chart, test one point of each triangle (one triangle at a time) and ask:

Does this triangle need balancing and/or stabilizing? (Test)

If the test is positive, one or more of the points and/or links of that triangle is in need of balancing and/or stabilizing. Identify which point(s) and/or link(s) are involved. Do this by either touching or focusing on a specific point or link and asking:

Is it this point/link? (Test)

Whatever tests positive is the weak spot. Example:

green beans — zucchini — sweet banana peppers — Point 2 (zucchini) and link 3 (between the peppers and green beans) may test weak.

3. You will do a soil balancing and stabilizing for *each* weak point and/or link.* (Usually there will be only one weak area in any given triangle. I have not yet found more than two weak areas. In the above example, you would balance and stabilize point 2 and link 3.) For each weak point/link ask:

What balancers are needed? (Test your soil balancing kit.)

Then connect with Pan (verify your connection), place a small amount of each balancer needed into your hand or a spoon, and ask Pan to shift the energy appropriately to the point or link you are working with. Use the same process to work with Pan as you would in a soil balancing. Then ask:

What stabilizers are needed? (Test the flower essences.)

Place 1 drop of each needed essence in your hand (or a spoon) and repeat your work with Pan for the shift.

4. Repeat step 3 for each triangle that tests weak.

5. When all the triangles are balanced and stabilized, you can verify that you are finished by asking:

Are all the triangles' points in the garden balanced and stabilized? (Test)

If you get a negative, go through the points again to find the one that was missed, and balance and stabilize that triangle using step 3. Then ask the above question again. This time you should get a positive.

When you get a positive, ask:

Are all the triangles' links balanced and stabilized? (Test)

If you get a negative, just go back as you did for the points that tested negative, and balance and stabilize the link that is still weak. Repeat the verification question until you get a positive.

6. Close the coning after thanking the team, and test yourself for essences and check for dosage.

* Do both the balancing and stabilizing of a point or link before addressing a second point or link. Don't balance all points or links needing work, then stabilize them all. Balancing and stabilizing are two stages of one unit of action and should be done together.

Also, work around the triangle sequentially. That is, point 1 > link 1 > point 2 > link 2 > point 3 > link 3. Don't work points 1, 2 and/or 3, then go back and work links 1, 2 and/or 3.

PLANT
TRIANGULATION
Once you do the first triangle balance in the spring, you will need to balance those triangles again only occasionally. It is easy to check for triangle balance during the regular garden meetings with nature that I discuss in chapter 10. Or, if a row or area suddenly shows signs of being in trouble, one of the first things to check for with nature is whether the plants in trouble are part of a triangle and if that triangle needs balancing.

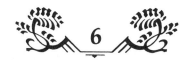

Flower Essences
Foliar Feeding

This is a very simple process (and I can hear you saying, "It's about time!"). Instead of using fish emulsion or liquid kelp or some such thing to spray on plant leaves for quick fertilizing, you use flower essences.

For those of you who don't know, plants absorb nutrients through the leaf surfaces up to 20 times faster than through their roots. Regular foliar feeding or leaf feeding is done by mixing a foliar feeding concentrate with water, adding a squirt of liquid soap to the water to "wet" it (this helps the spray stick to leaf surfaces better) and spraying this solution on plant leaves.

Flower essences foliar feeding uses the same process as regular foliar feeding, except that the concentrate used in the solution is flower essences instead of liquid kelp.

As you are moving your garden through the growing season, it would be good to periodically check to see if anything needs to be foliar fed with flower essences. If, for example, the green bean row tests positive, you would do the following:

1. Connect with the deva of the plant(s) involved. Verify your connection.

You do not need to open a coning for this information. However, if you already have a coning activated for something else and decide to check for flower essences foliar feeding needs, simply add to the coning the deva of the plant variety that tested positive for the feeding. You will work with each variety separately, adding that variety's deva to the coning while you get the information and disconnecting from that deva *before* going on to the next variety and its deva. In short, don't try to pile all the devas you'll need into the coning at one time. Bring each deva into the 4-point coning as you need it.

2. Ask:
   Does _____ need flower essence foliar feeding? (Test)

3. If yes, ask:
   What flower essences does _____ need? (Test the essences.)
Pull out any bottles that test positive. Check your result by placing the bottles that tested positive in your lap and asking:
   Are these the essences that are needed? (Test)
If you did not get a positive, check your solution by first asking if there are additional essences that should be included in the solution. If yes, test the sets of essences again and add the new bottles to the solution. Then, ask if any essences that are part of the solution should now be excluded. (You may have accidently tested positive for a bottle that should have been a negative.) If yes, test each solution bottle individually, asking if that bottle is to be included in the solution. What tests negative gets removed. Now test your solution as a whole. This time it should test positive.

4. Get a modified dosage by asking:
   How many drops of each essence are to be added to this spray container of water?
(A quart spray bottle, a 5-liter spray tank or whatever size you are using. Just be certain of the size container you'll be using.)
Then ask:
   Do I spray in early morning or early evening?
(Foliar feeding is done either in the early morning hours or in the late afternoon/early evening hours when the energy in the plant leaves is highest.)

Finally, ask:

For how many days do I spray these plants?

(Rarely will you test to spray more than 1 time. Flower essences foliar feeding is very efficient.)

5. Disconnect from the deva and connect with the next deva regarding another plant variety you wish to check. Then repeat steps 2, 3 and 4.

6. When you have all of your information, disconnect from the last deva or close down the full coning. If you were in coning, test yourself for essences and check for dosage.

7. Mix the drops of essences in the spray bottle or tank. Add a little liquid soap—I add about 1/2 teaspoon per 5 liters of water. If the spray beads up on the leaves and runs off, add a little more soap. Spray the plants, including the underside of the leaves, as well. Foliar feeding (regular or flower essences) should not be done on a rainy day.

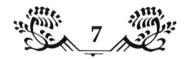

Insect Balancing
Process

My relationship with the insects in the Perelandra garden environment has grown and changed since I began co-creative gardening in 1976. During the first year, as described in *Behaving As If the God In All Life Mattered*, I worked with the devas in ways that taught me that insects were indeed an important part of the garden and could just as easily be worked with co-creatively as the plants. After that first year, and up until 1988, the insect patterns and rhythms were not addressed directly, and the insects were given free run of the garden. I noticed quickly that as the garden plants and soil were balanced, the insects struck a comparable balance automatically.

In 1988, I felt a shift in how I was to work with the insects in the garden. For the first time since 1976, nature suggested that I hand-pick some insects from their plants. This began a series of changes that have led from a benign, non-direct relationship with the insects to a deeper, new co-creative partnership and to the two insect energy processes.

When I first got the sense to make a change in my relationship with the insects, I questioned these changes in my weekly garden meeting with the nature intelligences. The following is what I was told.

Although most "bugs" which we see in a garden are insects, the adults of which have six legs, I use the word "insect" to include other creatures such as centipedes, millipedes and arachnids (spiders, mites, ticks, etc. which have eight legs).

GARDEN SESSION
Garden Coning—28 June 1988

Machaelle: I sense that it was OK to gently remove by hand some of the squash bugs and place them in a section of the meadow in an effort to offer them an alternative. Is this correct, or should I maintain the policy of not interfering with the insects?

Coning: You have a viable partnership with the insects of the garden as well as the plants and soil. This you know. We suggest that if you would like to offer alternatives that you work directly with the nature spirits tending the insects in the area in question. Balance will be the major consideration. Should an alternative be one that maintains balance for all concerned, the nature spirits will inform you. Then you can respond accordingly.

As to the squash bugs that you moved to the meadow last night: The gentleness and concern you demonstrated towards the squash bugs went a considerable distance in healing the rift that has developed between these insects and humankind. In the case in question, the meadow alternative does not address the needs of the insects. It is best that the squash bugs that are drawn to the squash plants remain with the plants. However, because of the heartfelt concern you demonstrated towards them, you will see a much stronger balance maintained between plant and insect. You need not worry about the welfare of the insects you moved to the meadow. They shortly found their way back to the plants!

As you feel inclined, it would be most beneficial to the insect kingdom as a whole if you would make similar gestures of the heart that would serve to demonstrate in both intent and action a new partnership between insects and humans at Perelandra. Just from the overall direction and intent of Perelandra, and especially in the garden, much healing has already occurred and continues to occur. But demonstrations of your intent and gestures such as those shown last evening will enhance that healing process. You need not will yourself to enter into an intense "gesture process" with the insects. Simply follow the pull of your heart and mind. And check with the nature spirits about the appropriateness of relocating some insects to other areas of the garden environment.

In 1989, my relationship with insects changed again with the introduction of the Flower Essences Foliar Feeding Process. And again, I raised some questions about these developments in the weekly garden meeting with the nature intelligences.

GARDEN SESSION
Garden Coning—29 June 1989

You have asked several questions about the garden that we would like to address now—the first question being the purpose behind the flower essence foliar feeding process that was introduced this week.

*All of the various energy balancing processes that have been used in the garden are designed to balance the garden environment according to the needs of **all** the various "members" who are a part of the environment as a whole. The focus is not solely on the vegetables, herbs and flowers. A true garden environment is never reduced to the vegetables, herbs and flowers growing in it. A garden environment is a larger phenomenon that includes these three elements.*

The intent of vegetable gardens is food production. (We recognize that the intent of the Perelandra garden is primarily research, but food production by definition is still included.) This intent—food production—is an overriding factor that permeates the entire garden environment. It relates not just to human need, but to the needs of all elements that are a part of the overall environment. Hence, the importance of insects. A garden environment could never be balanced without the inclusion of insects. As they move through their life cycle with the plants, insects become a part of the food production for countless birds, reptiles and even the insects themselves. So you will not see the Perelandra garden without a healthy, vibrant population of insects as long as it is balanced. The energy balancing processes you have done in the garden—the Battle Energy Release, the Energy Cleansing Process, the Soil Balancing Process—all have been done to assure a complete balancing of the garden environment.

Now you ask, why doesn't all this energy balance work assure a balanced interaction between insect and plant? It does. The activity you have observed such as the egg clusters on the squash plant leaves is well within the balance of the plants themselves. The plants are serving these insects as a unique hatchery. Don't forget, the insects must be present if the overall environment is to be balanced. The structure, shape, timing and rhythm of the squash plant, and the other varieties belonging to the squash plant family, serve this specific insect-hatching process extremely well. As you have noted many times, nature is not stupid. It will choose the conditions that best serve it. Consequently, you see the squash bug utilizing the squash plant as a hatchery.

The flower essence foliar feeding is not for the purpose of thwarting this activity in the least. You will notice that it was not used until after the primary egg-laying activity had concluded. On the contrary, the Perelandra garden environment is so rich and vital that you will find a need for a high population of insects as part of the support system. What the new essences foliar feeding is accomplishing is a **dispersion** of specific insect populations from one small area of the environment—in this case we refer to the five squash plants—into the garden environment as a whole.

An appropriate hatchery does not mean that it can support the full life cycle. It implies only that it can successfully support the hatchery needs. The essence foliar feeding is quickly enhancing the energy of the plants in such a way as to encourage the newly hatched insects to disperse throughout the entire garden environment. Any population of insects that is perfectly in balance with the Perelandra garden environment as a whole would quickly overwhelm any one plant variety if those plants were to provide the sole life sustenance for the insects.

When overall garden environments are not balanced, the insects will seek the proper hatchery conditions but will remain closely connected to that hatchery because the insects will sense safety there that is not present in the full environment. Of course that sense of safety is an illusion. The hatchery plants cannot support a full lifetime for any one population of insects; and humans, in their attempt to "save the hatchery" for their own food needs, have taken to using lethal chemicals on the plants. In the organic gardening approach, the focus has been on discouraging the insects from using the garden plants as a hatchery in the first place. But, although this may solve the human need without introducing hazardous chemicals into an already fragile environment, it does not address the need for insects to be fully present within a balanced garden environment. And other "members" either suffer, leave or become extinct within their own environment. This then results in imbalance, which ultimately reflects back on the vitality level of the food that humans are eating from the garden, causing human sustenance to be compromised.

When any member or element of nature is forced to alter its pattern—

that pattern which originates from the devic level—for survival purposes on a long-term basis, it ultimately alters the natural devic pattern. This is part of the co-creative process built into the species itself. An environmental shift that causes a long-term survival response will attach itself to the original devic pattern and become a part of the overall devic weave.

The insect population within a garden setting has for quite some time refused to disperse into the larger environment from its hatchery areas. It has sensed the larger environment to be hostile. And it has been correct. This reluctance to disperse has resulted in the hatchery areas also becoming hostile due to the human attempt to control insect activity. The insects, sensing outside environmental hostility, have simply chosen to stay put and fight for survival. This has gone on for so long that the devic patterns in the various gardening and farming insect populations have altered. The natural pattern now includes remaining close to the hatchery environment. The flower essence foliar feeding is a co-creative device, shall we say, for encouraging dispersal. Over a period of time, the insect survival pattern will once again shift, and the insects will automatically disperse throughout the whole garden environment—and the essence foliar feeding, as it is used for this purpose, will no longer be necessary.

Something else we'd like to point out: Until now, we have not moved with you to encourage this insect dispersal. Instead, we have maintained focus on the overall state of balance in the garden environment. This has required a step-by-step healing process that has gone on these past nine years.

The garden environment itself has reached a high level of balance and is inviting to the insect population. Over the years, it has become less and less a threat to insect survival. Many things have been done within that environment not only to improve balance but also to prepare the environment for the eventual insect dispersal. There had to be friendly, life-sustaining "facilities" added that would encourage and hold the insect dispersal. For example, one of the purposes of the meadow and the newly planted wildflower area was preparation for the eventual insect dispersal. In short, before making moves to activate the insects to disperse, their surrounding environment was prepared. Often humans, when attempting to environmentally balance an area, will work in the reverse—demand dispersal and then clamor, usually without success, to do something that will support the change after it's been made. This results in failure in the human effort and disaster for whatever has been dispersed.

On to the practical level: Throughout this growing season, essence foliar feeding will be used to shift the plant energy and encourage dispersal. At first you will see increased insect activity throughout the garden. They will be reluctant to leave the garden proper. We realize, as do you, that if left alone, this will only serve to destroy other areas of the garden. The dispersal must be throughout the entire garden environment in order to assure balance. Using the essence foliar feeding process, we will gently encourage complete dispersal. So you may see some plant varieties left "vulnerable" in the garden. They will be luring the insects in an outward fashion. And then the next week, these plants will be foliar fed in order to encourage further outward dispersal. You will also see a greater influx of activity from those members of nature who naturally interact with the insects. This activity also will disperse into the larger whole as the insects move out. Throughout all of this, you will note the health, vibrancy and production of the hatchery plants, for they will no longer be used for the insects' total life-cycle needs.

One last point: Just as a hostile environment has prevented insects from moving out from their hatchery areas, that same sense of hostile environment has prevented the members of nature who interact with these insects from entering the hatchery areas. Don't forget that the hatchery areas have become stages for "warfare" conducted by the human gardener in an attempt to save the plants for his food needs. As a consequence, a virtual banquet of insects has been left alone.

In a co-creative garden, this reluctance to interact is broken down. What one sees almost immediately is an increase in wildlife activity in and around the garden. With the insect dispersal, that activity will increase tenfold. The natural interaction is increased when there is activity and movement rather than inactivity. The more the insects disperse, the healthier they will become, since their life-cycle needs will be more fully met, and the more interaction they will attract from all who depend on the insects for life sustenance because of their eye-catching activity and action.

I continued the flower essence foliar feeding throughout the 1989 growing season and, indeed, the insects dispersed in a dramatic fashion. In fact, some insects completely left their hatchery plants and moved throughout the garden. I noticed that once they dispersed, the larger collection of garden plants could easily handle the insect interaction. Other insects, like the squash bugs, would disperse throughout the garden during the day and would return to the squash and zucchini plants at night. I lost those plants, but no others, to the squash bug activity. Also, the squash bugs continued returning to the squash and zucchini plants even when there was nothing left to the plants but a dead, brown, main stem. I was told not to remove these ugly hulks, and the squash bugs continued using them as "central gathering stations" throughout their life cycle in the growing season.

At the end of the 1989 growing season and during the early months of 1990, the two insect energy processes were developed and, I must say, my relationship with insects was forever changed—again.

The first insect energy process I call the "Insect Balancing Process." It uses the flower essences and, while linked with the devic level of the various species of insects, one species at a time—squash bug, cabbage moth/worm, cabbage looper, etc.—the process balances and strengthens the insects. It is a healing process geared specifically to the insects. It utilizes the same concepts used in soil balancing and atmospheric balancing in that the nature spirit level is working with us to release the flower essences' energy to the insects.

INSECT BALANCING PROCESS STEPS

Use only the flower essences for this process. You will be balancing only. Make a list of the insect species that are common in your garden.

1. Open a 4-point coning. Balance and stabilize the coning and check yourself for essences.

2. State that you want to do the Insect Balancing Process. Using the list of garden insects in your area, test to find out what insects you are to work with.

If you can't identify an insect properly and don't know its name, make up one. Connect with that insect (just picture it in your mind) and let it know that when you say "_____," you mean that specific insect species. For example, I call one type of insect the "Perelandra Lunar Landing Module" or "LLM" because it looks like a lunar landing module.

An option to this approach is to request that any insects that need balancing come to your mind *sequentially*. When you are ready to begin, ask the first insect to "come" to you.

Beginning with the first insect species on your list or the first insect species that pops into mind, ask to be connected in the coning to the deva of that species. Verify your connection.

3. Ask:

What essences are needed for strengthening and balancing this species?

Test the essences. Pull out any bottles that test positive. Check your test as you would any flower essence solution.

4. Place 1 drop of each essence needed in your hand or a spoon.

5. Hold out the essence and state to Pan:

I ask that Pan shift the energy of the essence solution and make it available to these insects in the appropriate concentration.

Continue to hold out the solution for about 10 seconds for the energy shift to occur. Verify that the work is completed. Clean your hand or the spoon.

6. Disconnect from the deva of this group of insects. (Verify that you are disconnected.) Ask to be connected to the next species or group. Just move to the next one on the list or request that the next species pop into your mind.

Repeat steps 3 through 6 until no other insect species pops into mind or is left on your list. Disconnect from the last deva you were working with.

In step 7, you work with the insects as a mixed group. The essences will be released to this group.

7. For a final test, ask to be connected with the Overlighting Deva of Insects. (Verify your connection.) Ask:

Are any essences needed for collective balancing and strengthening of the remainder of the insect population who are a part of the garden environment? (Test)

If yes, repeat steps 3 through 5, asking Pan to shift the energy of the solution to this larger group. Hold out the solution for 10 seconds and verify that the shift has occurred.

8. Disconnect from the Overlighting Deva of Insects and, after thanking the team, close down the 4-point coning. Verify that it is closed. Test yourself for essences and a dosage.

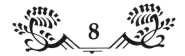

Insect Triangulation

The second insect process I call the "Insect Triangulation Balancing Process." This one balances and stabilizes the interrelationship among a specific group of insects, the specific variety of plants they are interfacing with and the gardener. The insects, plants and gardener create three points, and we have an energy link among them, the same as three plants in a triangle. Using kinesiology, we can discern whether this triangle is balanced or not and, if it is not, which point or link in the triangle is weak and needs balancing and stabilizing. So, in a triangle formed among the squash bug, the squash plants and me, all of the points may test strong. But once the links between the three points are tested, I could discover that the link between me, as the gardener, and the squash bug is in need of balancing and stabilizing. Any weak point or link in this triangulation is balanced using the same balancers you use in the soil balancing and then stabilized using flower essences.

I have to tell you that when I completed the first Insect Triangulation Process, all my insects, in triangulation, needed the link between them and me balanced and stabilized. The minute I completed the balancing and stabilizing, I felt the insect was suddenly free and able, for the first time, to leave the garden. I realized that one of the keys to the concentration of insects in a garden is this weak link between the gardener and them, and that the insects are unable to disperse or leave until that link is balanced and stabilized. The concept of triangulation among the insect, the plant and the gardener made sense to me because I saw that it was on the plants that we gardeners focus our expectations for both the plant and the insect.

This process can be done separately or back to back with the Insect Balancing Process. Also, since you are working with both plant varieties and insect species in this process, there will be more testing done than with other processes—especially in the beginning. You can do this process over a period of days, spending only as long as your energy level holds up each day. With my first round of testing, it took me a total of four days to complete the task. Each day you will open a coning, set yourself up and begin where you left off.

INSECT TRIANGULATION PROCESS STEPS

Have your flower essences and soil balancing kit handy.

1. Open a 4-point coning. Balance and stabilize the coning and check yourself for essences.

2. From the list you made of the insect species that were balanced in the previous process, test to find out which insects need a triangle balancing. Just ask:

Which insects need a triangle balancing?! (Test)

Just getting this list ready for the triangulation testing can take a day or two. So, relax and pace yourself well. This is a terrific process to do in February! Believe me, it's worth the effort.

3. Move through this insect list, one species at a time. Now, with each insect species, you will need to find out which plant varieties are involved in weak triangles. For example, with the squash bug, I tested that I would have to do triangulation work with the bug *and* watermelon, crispy melon, yellow summer squash, zucchini, cantaloupe and cucumber. That's a total of 6 triangulation balancing and stabilizing tests for one bug. To get the plant list, I used my common sense and tested each of the plant varieties I knew these insects interact with. Then I asked if there were any additional plants. Rarely did I get a yes, but when I did, I just moved through the garden chart row by row to locate the row of the mystery plant, and then tested each of that row's varieties to locate the plants.

Then I added that plant to the list for the specific insect I was working with.

4. First, to prepare the insect species for the triangulation process, add to the coning the species' deva and do a balancing and stabilizing for the insect. That is, ask what balancers are needed (use your soil kit balancers) and administer a small amount to the insects through Pan, and repeat this process by asking what stabilizers are needed, using the flower essences.

If no balancers or stabilizers are needed, the insects are already prepared and you can move on to step 5.

5. Still keeping the insect's deva in the coning, connect with the deva of the specific plant variety. Verify your connection. So, now you have the devas of the insect and the plant variety added to the 4-point coning. Do a regular triangulation process. To keep this straight, I wrote down:

Squash Bug — Zucchini — Me —

"Squash Bug," "Zucchini" and "Me" are the points of the triangle and "—" represents the links. Then I tested point #1, link #1, point #2, link #2, point #3, link #3. I did a balancing and stabilizing on whatever tested weak, using Pan's assistance to shift the balancers and stabilizers to the appropriate point and link. For the above triangle, the link between the squash bug and me tested weak, and with Pan's help, it was balanced with rock phosphate and manganese, and stabilized with the Perelandra Rose Essence, Gruss an Aachen.

When you have completed testing one triangle, disconnect the plant's deva from the coning and connect with the next plant's deva in the next triangle. You will be working with the same insect and each of its plants from the list—plus you, the gardener.

HINT: To see patterns developing and understand how this process unfolds in the garden, I suggest that you keep notes on all testing for each insect variety and its triangles. *In fact, in order to see the wisdom of all the energy processes and to watch how they unfold and interweave, I suggest you keep notes on all the testing.*

6. Once you have completed work on all the triangles involving one insect species, disconnect the deva of that species from the coning (and the deva of the last plant you worked with, if you haven't

already done so) and connect with the deva of the next insect species. Verify your connection. Then repeat steps 4 and 5.

Continue doing this until you have tested all the insect species with all their triangles. Some plants will interact with more than one insect species and will be a part of several triangles—a separate triangle for each of the insect species. Do the balancing and stabilizing testing for each triangle.

7. At the end of each testing session, thank the team, disconnect from the last insect and plant devas you were working with and close down the 4-point coning. Also, check yourself again for flower essences and a dosage.

These two insect energy processes completely changed my attitude toward and understanding of insects and their interaction in the garden. I found that I could not be connected with the insects' devas and not feel a closer and more intimate connection with insects as a whole. Instead of feeling on the outside looking in, as far as insects were concerned, I now feel an intimate link and kinship with this level of life. Just this shift in attitude alone impacted the insects in the Perelandra garden. Their movements and rhythms altered dramatically and I found I didn't know how to observe these changes! They were so different, I simply didn't know how to perceive what was happening.

Also, in the beginning of this year's growing season, the rhythm of the insects in the garden itself and the rhythm of the insects in the garden environment as a whole were quite similar. Then in mid-July, the garden insect activity changed dramatically again while the insects interfacing with the surrounding garden environment remained the same. Now I was totally lost as to what I was seeing, so I opened a garden coning and asked for clarification.

GARDEN SESSION
Garden Coning + Overlighting Deva of Insects—26 July 1990

Machaelle: What I would like is some insight about what is going on in the garden regarding insect rhythms and patterns and what approach you suggest I use in working with the insects. I'm a bit lost right now and I feel this is because I am looking at the insect movements through old eyes and with old expectations. I need help in seeing what I need to see in order not to interfere with what is to happen with the insects. Am I making myself clear?

Coning: Perfectly. First of all, let us state to you again that the insect population in the garden is not out of balance nor out of control when looking at the entire garden environmental balance. Most often, when people look at a garden, they see only the plants that grow in that garden. They define a garden by those plants. This leads them to a limited and narrow understanding of what a garden is, and this perspective is at the core of the problem when discussing garden imbalances and questions of garden productivity.

When humans developed the concept of organized planting for food needs, they actually were developing not a garden or a farm but, rather, an overall environment in which organized food production would be and could be supported. From our perspective, these environments, be they small gardens or large-scale farms, are complex self-sustaining realities that must, if they are to function well, be in balance within themselves and in balance with the larger environment of which they are a part. This is not an easy task. The difficulty that humans have experienced in developing an effective food production environment serves to illustrate our point.

We might digress here for just a minute to point out that the period of food production over the past fifty years in which man has relied on chemical manipulation for "success" has shown that such manmade manipulation will appear to have short-term success but will never be a long-term answer. Humans have had to see for themselves the shortcomings of such manipulation. In essence, humans have had to see just how far their creative and mental prowess can take them regarding nature and how little it gives them in the end. No amount of words from us of nature or the wisest of humans could have served to teach the lessons humans are now learning about the shortcomings of their own manipulations.

We in nature do not see the past fifty years of chemical and manmade development from the standpoint of disaster and destructive failure. Surely its impact has been such. But rather, we see these years and the experiences they have given as deep lessons that have served to lay a foundation for the necessary changes of the present and future. Man must understand why he acts and what purpose his actions will serve, or he will sense himself to be in a void. These lessons, as difficult as they may be, serve to teach purpose and will become the very foundation of the new relationship between man and nature. So, although damage has been suffered by both humans and nature due to the chemical-manipulation thrust of the past fifty years, we in nature do not see this time as a waste or as destruction leading to a dead end.

We would like to point out, however, that these experiences and lessons that humans are now waking up to and acknowledging were not initiated by and designed by nature for human education. They are, as the lessons themselves so clearly demonstrate, of human making, human design and human initiation. We only wish to point out that although humans are waking up to the destruction they have created and are feeling anger, despair and, in some cases, guilt about this destruction, we of nature see it as an opportunity to lay a strong, deep, stable foundation for the new way in which humans understand why they relate to nature and form different- ly. They will then not be like children being led into the future blindly, but responsible, thinking adults capable of creating a vibrant and life-giving partnership with nature.

*Returning to the garden environment: As we have said, we see these environments as complex, self-sufficient realities requiring careful and full balance in order to function well. As indicated in the Workbook and in your subsequent research, this entails a great many facets and levels of environmental development—both seen and unseen. From the perspective of the whole, the presence of plants that are placed by humans to initiate such environments is minor when looking at all other aspects and facets that environment must include for self-sustaining balance. Placement of the plants serves only to give us of nature a definition of precisely what the environment is to be. To say that you are planning a garden or even a vegetable garden only **begins** to define such an environment. However, to actually choose the plants desired and, as in the past, prior to the advent of co-creative partnership with nature, to actually place those plants within the desired area gives the human-intended definition we need in order to then establish, or try to establish, the balanced, self-sustaining environment required to support the human-intended garden. In short, humans initiate* *and act on their desire for a specialized environment, and we in nature then move to create the surrounding balanced, self-sustaining support for that environment.*

We have not been able to work in concert with humans up to the advent of the co-creative partnership processes. It has been a situation in which we have had to attempt to shore up and create life balance around human demand. In some cases, where the humans involved have been more open to intuitive input, we have had limited success. In other cases, where humans have looked to sources of outside control for assistance and the illusion of success, we have not been successful. It might be interesting to you to note that where there has been an illusion of success, it has been focused on the plants around which the garden was created. The human never expanded into recognizing anything other than those plants. "Success" has been defined by how satisfied the human is regarding those specific plants.

*Now, with the co-creative partnership, humans can initiate the creation of a specialized environment and then work **with** nature to establish such an environment in a balancing and healing process from the very beginning, at the point of initiation. We in nature will not initiate such specialized environments. We do not, as an overall, interactive nature dynamic need them. We only work to establish them once they have been initiated by humans. By definition, from the point of inception, we have a partnership. And instead of nature being relegated to a position in the rear in which it is forced to come in behind human desire and will in order to set up or attempt to set up an environment that can best support the human desire and will, nature can work alongside humans and establish these environments in balance with human desire and will from the beginning.*

As we have said, the plants that are the focal point for human desire and will regarding specialized environments are only a small part of those environments. But from our perspective, they give us the definition and direction for creating the environment. If humans could see, could perceive all of the elements that must come together to create a self-sustaining environment, it would resemble to them a fair-sized city with a comparable management complexity. As with a city, time and development are never stagnant. Change is ever-present. Consequently, the balances between and among the various elements are constantly shifting to accommodate the change.

When we work with humans directly, we are able to quickly establish an environmental foundation from which to build, depending upon which directions for growth, change and development the garden intent takes, and we are able to accommodate these changes effortlessly. The complex order and organization that are required take on a sense of carefully designed patterns and rhythms. If we are relegated to a position of constantly coming in behind human will and desire in a support effort, you will see what resembles breakdown and chaos, because human will and desire will always be one step or more ahead of nature creation. The two will not be in sync.

In order for you to understand the co-creative gardening/farming processes and how they are being demonstrated at Perelandra, it is important that you have a clearer sense of the complexity of the environment in which you are working. For many years, you have been primarily concerned—because this has been where we have directed you—with the specific plants that have served to define the Perelandra garden environment. That is, you have been concerned with the various vegetables, flowers, fruits and herbs that "make up" the garden. From this, you have expanded that initial focus to include soil, and then garden animals, birds and insects, and then surrounding land such as the woods-edge and wildflower triangles. Constantly, your focus has expanded. You have recognized and touched into the various main areas that serve to make up this specialized environment. What we have learned together has created the Perelandra Garden Workbook and given people the access and information needed for creating a balanced, fully functioning, specialized environment.

We have now entered a new stage of the Perelandra garden—and we use the word "garden" to include all activities that serve to define the intent and thrust of the physical Perelandra garden itself. So do not limit what we say to exclude the various avenues of research, development and outreach. We refer you back to your moving on to the next level of research. As we have said, and as you have come to realize, this has moved you and Perelandra to a completely new level of operation and activity. The intent of the garden has broadened to include deeper areas of research. This includes the interaction with you from the perspective of nature.

In order to best facilitate such phenomena as the creation of specialized environments, we need the Perelandra laboratory. From it, we work with you to discover and develop ways in which specialized environments can be established that will promote a self-sustaining balance and strengthen the *overall balance of the whole. It is the Perelandra laboratory that gives us the opportunity to work out the co-creative processes needed throughout the rest of the planet, as well as by the rest of the various levels and dimensions working within the band of form.*

*Co-creative processes must be developed for the multitude of **all** elements that make up a specialized environment. It is a complete partnership that is needed, not a limited one that focuses only on a small number of plants. When a human wishes to create a flower garden, those flowers only serve to define the direction of the garden. They do not constitute the full extent of the co-creative partnership. The partnership must be extended to include all elements that are required for the specialized environment. In short, the gardener becomes, along with nature, the co-manager of a city.*

As the level of operation around research and development has deepened in the Perelandra garden environment, you have observed two areas of change. One has been the dramatic increase in animal, reptile and insect activity in the environment. This increase has been a part of the physical structural changes that have occurred in order that the new level of Perelandra garden work be appropriately supported. In Perelandra's case, the specialized environment is that of a scientific laboratory for discovering and disseminating processes that will allow humans and nature to work together in a balanced co-creative partnership. The increase in wildlife within the laboratory environment has occurred to support the change in intent regarding the deeper work.

Another change has been in a specific area of the research—insects. We are focusing our attention at present on the patterns and rhythms of the vast insect population that must be present in a specialized environment such as Perelandra and in gardens in general.

If you could see the Perelandra garden environment as a physical laboratory with furniture instead of plants and wildlife, you would see that the central laboratory bench upon which the research is done would be what is now the garden proper. It is here that we concentrate our research work. The rest of the garden environment could be characterized as the laboratory facilities and structure that protect and support the work being done at the bench. If you see a change in natural pattern and rhythm in the garden proper—the 100-foot area—you can pretty much be assured that this change relates directly to the specific work going on in the laboratory. The results of this work would then benefit the whole, through both the outreach program that has developed at Perelandra and from us as we develop co-creative partnerships with other humans. The level and range of our input regarding matters stemming from the partnership will be adjusted according to the work and findings we experience at Perelandra.

If there is a change in pattern and rhythm in, for example, the woods-edge, or the grassy areas, or the new meadow, woods or cabin area, this would be due to a need to alter and adjust the physical supportive structure of the laboratory to enhance a new level of the work going on. As you notice changes in these two areas—the laboratory bench and the structure itself—you are welcome to check with us to make sure that what you observe falls into the above-mentioned categories so that they may be approached by you accordingly.

When you consider the balance that is being created at the Perelandra laboratory, it is limiting to feel that the only balance is that which is apparent in the garden proper, the laboratory bench. To appreciate the Perelandra garden balance, one must see the balance being demonstrated throughout the entire laboratory environment. That is, after all, what supports and stabilizes the laboratory-bench work. To help you understand the depth of the Perelandra garden environment balance, we would like to point out to you (a) this year's development around the gypsy moths [We had a heavy infestation that then nearly disappeared due to natural predators.], (b) the marked increase in wildlife being drawn to the environment and (c) the changes that have occurred in the new field around the wildflower increase and the wildlife increase. These are all examples of strength and balance. The Perelandra laboratory could not sustain this kind of increase in life vitality if it were not for the strong, deep health and balance of the laboratory itself. Life will not attract to non-life.

As we have said, we in nature have been concentrating for these past two growing seasons, in particular, on insect interaction within a garden environment. To do this, we have included in the devic plan specific insect rhythms and patterns that give us the opportunity to work with you on processes for both healing and balancing. To be honest with you, the insect patterning you observe in the Perelandra garden laboratory proper does not resemble the ebb and flow of the insect patterns in the rest of the Perelandra environment. For the purpose of the work, we have speeded up, altered and shifted these patterns to accommodate the research that is needed. All of these changes are both special and part of the devic balance in light of the Perelandra laboratory opportunity.

There may be years when certain insect activity will more than defy logic. For example, this year you observed little insect activity on the bean rows until three weeks ago. Now you have rows that have the kind of insect activity one would call problematic. We needed for this to occur to continue work that was begun last season on processes for insect balancing and healing. As this season continues, you will see other shifts that defy observable logic in these rows. This will be due to both the results of the developing processes and the fact that this part of the testing is complete. The rows will now be returned to a more balanced pattern and rhythm. It will appear that the rows in question will be making 180 degree turns on a dime. In short, this is precisely what they will be doing.

The work in the garden laboratory will continue to take these sharp and illogical turns because of the kind of research that is now occurring and will continue to occur for some time. People who visit the garden more than once will be more likely to see these turn-arounds. Others, who only have a one-time chance to observe the garden, will not understand all they see. But they will pick up and experience a strong, balanced energy environment unlike anything they have felt. This will occur because the Perelandra laboratory is balanced—to a depth unlike anything they have ever experienced. The experiments are also balanced. But, due to the fact that visitors are looking at experiments in progress, what they see happening at the time may seem questionable. They may not understand or be able to perceive the kind of balance being demonstrated in the experiments themselves. In short, they may perceive chaos when, in fact, they are looking at controlled, deliberately designed "chaos"—or research—that is in balance with the surrounding environment and the global environment. They are not looking at destruction. They are looking at balanced, controlled research and development. Despite what they see, or think they see, they will experience a feeling of health and balance beyond anything they could have imagined.

You have already begun to expand the various areas of testing that you do for the weekly phase 3 meetings. We concur that it is now advisable to include the Overlighting Deva of Insects for input in that meeting. This will keep you informed about the insect balance in both the laboratory bench areas and the surrounding laboratory. This addition will also facilitate the developing insect-balancing processes, for it is primarily through the weekly meetings that we set up with you those areas of work and testing that need to be done in partnership. From the results, we are then able to suggest changes until we have a process that is fully effective and ready to be released to others.

*We also suggest that the meeting include input regarding the Perelandra laboratory supporting structure **and** input regarding the laboratory bench. The readout you do with the present charts relates directly to the laboratory bench. You might wish to develop a chart that will list the various elements of the laboratory structure from which you will work during the meeting to get input as to its balance. On a whole, there is very little balancing work needed in these areas except during the early spring months. In essence, the laboratory is being prepared appropriately for stabilizing and supporting the coming laboratory bench work. But for your own records and information, you may wish to keep a separate listing of this work.*

One additional thought, unless you have any questions: You have received feedback from others who are developing co-creative partnerships, primarily in the area of gardening. You have been surprised at how efficiently and easily their partnership is going and how immediately effective are their results. You have joked that what has taken you 15 years to do is taking others 6 months or a year. As a joke, you have suggested that you are slow. When you have questioned others' quick and outstanding results, you have tended to explain your longer time and slower results as being a result of your not having the book. This is only part of the reason. Surely, your not having access to a book and having to develop a partnership "out of the blue" with us has been a factor.

But you have overlooked something else. Perelandra, since 1979, has been a fully functioning laboratory. For the sake of the research and development, it has been designed to take on more difficult, tricky and complex situations. In actuality, for years the garden proper has not closely resembled the patterns and rhythms usually found in family gardens. In comparison, what occurs in and is involved with a family garden is quite simple.

We have utilized the Perelandra laboratory to extend research and development in areas outside the garden environment that are more complex yet still related to the principles and dynamics expressed in a gar-den. Now, you already understand that the principles and dynamics ex-pressed in a garden are identical to those expressed in other areas where humans and nature come together—only the complexity differs. The Perelandra laboratory serves to establish the co-creative processes needed in a variety of areas where humans and nature either come together or need to come together in partnership. To extend this research, the complexity of the garden proper may be altered appropriately. The individual seeking to es-tablish a partnership with nature in a garden or farm situation would not come across this kind of complexity. In short, what we are saying is that the Perelandra garden cannot be accurately compared with other co-crea-tive gardens because it is not a garden. It is a co-creative scientific laboratory. However, you may judge the quality of the work going on at the Perelandra laboratory by the scope, depth, efficiency and effectiveness that others experience when they apply the processes coming out of Perelandra to their gardens, farms, landscaping, businesses, health and life.

Does this give you a better understanding of both the Perelandra lab and the insect activity?

Machaelle: Yes. And I feel I have a much better sense of working with the laboratory structure and at the laboratory bench. I think the weekly meetings will be much clearer, on my part, now. I have no further questions. You picked up on all my questions as we went along. If I come up with anything later, I'll reopen the session.

Coning: That will be fine. We suggest you close the coning now. It's been an especially long one but one in which you have held well.

Machaelle: Thank you.

Coning: You are most welcome. (Close coning.)

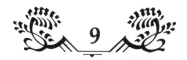

Calibration:
Finally, A Process
for the Gardener!

You're going to love this process. As the gardener, you are as much a part of the garden's balance and stability as the plants, atmosphere, soil and insects. I feel that there are two reasons why you're going to love this process. First of all, it is an extraordinarily simple and effective self-help tool. I think you will be amazed at the results this process will give you. Secondly, you will personally experience an energy process. You will therefore understand, from your experience, how the other energy processes impact and assist the plants, atmosphere, soil and insects. With their processes, you work with nature but you direct the focus of the process outside yourself. With the Calibration Process, you work with nature and direct the focus of the process to yourself. If you have any questions about whether or not these co-creative processes *really* work, you will not have those questions once you personally feel this energy process work and experience its results.

The following is the Perelandra Paper I did with nature on the Calibration Process.

SOME PERSONAL COMMENTS
ON THE CALIBRATION PROCESS

I have worked with this process extensively since I translated the Calibration Process session in March 1990. I wanted to understand and experience it before offering it to others, and I wanted to explore the different ways in which the process could be used. From the very first time I worked with it, I was amazed. I'd like to pass along to you some of my feelings about the process and give you ideas about when it can be used.

What impressed me first was the efficiency of the Calibration Process. It only takes a half-hour once you've explained the problem. Initially, I questioned this, not believing that so little time was needed to accomplish so much. In all of my work with the Calibration Process, the sessions have not exceeded the time it takes to express the problem and the half-hour. I'm quite used to nature coming up with exceptional co-creative processes that redefine the concepts of efficiency and effectiveness, but I was still impressed this time around.

It took a little thinking on my part to figure out when I was in a situation that could be helped by the Calibration Process. It is *not* needed if we are moving through an emotional or mental process where we have a sense of forward motion being maintained. It's useful when we feel our wheels spinning or feel stuck and can't even begin to imagine how we are to proceed—we're at a dead end. The Calibration Process doesn't sidestep us from emotional and mental processes. It is designed to keep our processes moving on all of our levels and "unjam" those places where we seem to have gotten stuck.

The first time I used the process in March 1990, I knew I was having difficulty addressing my work in the garden and maintaining focus on what I needed to do. I had tried every trick I knew that I thought might "wake me up." I might feel my ability to focus return, but it would be short-lived and I would quickly sink into what felt like a hole. I decided to try the Calibration Process. I set it up exactly as it is written in the session. I tried to explain as simply and succinctly as possible how I was feeling and how my life was being affected. And I admitted that I knew nothing else I could try. I sat for the half-hour and felt nothing happening. I closed the coning as instructed, assuming something would occur that would tip me off that I was now "healed" or whatever. Since I had done this session in the evening, I went about my "off hours" as usual. I still noticed nothing different by the time I went to bed. The next day, I began my day without thinking about either the process or possible changes. I just got on with what I had wanted to do. By the end of the day, it occurred to me that not only had I accomplished everything I could have hoped to do and more, but I had done all of this effortlessly. Not once did I feel I had to deliberately press myself through a project. I simply did it.

I wanted to share this first experience with you because it shows so clearly how the process can work without a bunch of bells and bugles sounding. In this instance, one day I was in one state of being (a difficult, unconstructive, wheel-spinning state) and the next day, after doing the process, I was in a completely different state of being. I didn't experience a linear progression from the first state to the next. I simply found myself in it. Sometimes I have found in this process that there aren't any great moments of understanding and resolution. At times I have felt that the gears between my emotional and mental levels and my body are simply "off" and in need of a little calibration. So, nature gets everything back into sync, and the dams that seem to cause the wheel-spinning unjam, and that's all it takes.

At other times, I did go through a resolution and understanding process that occurred either within the half-hour or within the twenty-four hours after the process. Again, it wasn't like some baseball bat hitting me in the head. Nothing that dramatic. I'd be moving along in my day and suddenly I'd know what the troublesome issue really was. Usually that in itself was the resolution. Or sometimes the resolution was in the form of action I needed to take to complete the issue.

I have used the Calibration Process when I was mentally buzzing and couldn't stop, when I couldn't stop working and when I could see that a fear I was experiencing was actually counter-productive and not helpful. Or, for some crazy reason, I found myself unable to make a decision even when I had all the information and input I needed. Another example: When I began the annual workshop series this year at Perelandra, I worked with the Calibration Process to shift me from my predominant role as the researcher to add the dynamic of the teacher. I found myself approaching and setting up the workshops in ways I had not even considered before—and it was better.

Everything I have experienced from this process verifies to me what nature says about the need to strike an involution/evolution balance within ourselves in order to function well. All my experiences have been accurate, efficient and effective. In working with the process, I have grown and developed around the area of emotional/mental balance in ways that allow me to more clearly see new areas where this process could be useful. If I suspect a Calibration Process would be helpful, I'll open the Healing Coning and ask: "Is this a situation that could be helped with the Calibration Process?"

So far, I've always been told yes.

UNDERSTANDING THE ISSUES HUMANS FACE AND WHY IT IS IMPERATIVE TO LINK IN CONSCIOUS PARTNERSHIPS WITH NATURE

It is becoming increasingly important for humans to understand the extensive partnership they have with nature, especially when focusing on issues of form and energy and all that this combination implies. We are presently in an interesting time in human development that has not been prevalent to this great extent at any other time. We refer to the fact that the desires and needs of the human soul on Earth completely outstrip the ability of the present support frameworks. By this we mean support frameworks in all areas: agricultural, scientific, physical health, mental and emotional health, governmental, social, educational . . . The development of the human soul collectively on Earth has surpassed the development of its support systems. In a nature-dominant environment that existed on the planet until the last fifty or so years, the human soul could more easily develop support systems that were compatible. One reason for this is that nature was abundant and could accommodate every human's needs. (We do not mean to imply that all needs were met, only that all needs could have been met had humans so chosen.) The physical means for all human support could have been met at any time because of natural abundance.

In the past fifty years, this balance has shifted and the planet has become human-dominant. Nature is no longer abundant enough to accommodate human needs and desires without careful consideration regarding the larger picture. We do not see this as a "bad" development. If ignored, however, it will be a dangerous development for all. But it is also a development that is forcing the human soul to expand on every level in order to address and survive the severe challenges that the shift to a human-dominant planet has created. Prior to this shift, individual human souls could expand and develop in ways that were not associated with survival. In short, there was a sense of leisure around the kind of expansion of which we speak. The individual had a lifetime to expand his understanding of life from a broader perspective while, at the same time, he devoted his efforts and energy primarily into those activities that served to support his day-to-day physical survival. Now, for the sake of survival on all levels, the human soul is required to make this shift, this expansion, and to do it quickly.

The present support systems were designed to best address human survival in a nature-dominant era that simultaneously existed within a Piscean context (parent/child emphasis). You are now seeing the shift to a human-dominant era that is simultaneously being impacted by the Aquarian impulses (partnership, balance and teamwork emphasis). All of the previously workable support systems are crumbling. At the same time, humans are expanding. By this we mean that the human in the conscious state is expanding to enfold the human spirit in the unconscious state. With this fusion, when it occurs, the unconscious becomes conscious. Humans are beginning to understand in an immediate and personal way that life is far broader and more complex than they ever before understood. This expansion does not occur in a vacuum. It requires support on all PEMS levels (physical, emotional, mental, spiritual) in order for it to be stabilized and maintained. So you have humans expanding in their efforts to address serious survival issues on all levels while, at the same time, having to function within a collection of frameworks that were never designed to meet the pressures of the present issues. There is an ever-expanding gap between today's expanding human and the planet's various social support systems' capabilities.

We have not gone off the topic of presenting the co-creative Calibration Process. We are giving you the background needed to understand the crux of the issues that humans face as well as why it is now so imperative for them to link in conscious partnerships with nature in order to develop the support systems of the future—and we mean by this the near-future!

The expansion of the human system requires that the expertise of nature in the areas of the relationship of form to energy and involution (bringing spirit and purpose into form) be tapped in direct proportion to the expansion. In your vernacular, the intensity and complexity of the game have increased to such a degree that the relative simplicity of the old support systems has been rendered ineffective. Humans must partner with nature in order to establish the systems that will support the new complexity. Don't forget—the expansion of the human consciousness to enfold its unconsciousness includes the grounding of the entire expansion into form. Otherwise, the expansion will either falter or take on an ungrounded air and be useless. This expansion process is what is referred to as "the evolution dynamic." The grounding of the expansion and its expression through form is what is meant by "the involution dynamic." The human soul is being pressed to open beyond or soar above the existing support systems on the planet in order to see the new. To properly support this expansion, the development of systems enfolding the balance between the involution dynamic and the evolution dynamic is imperative.

A reminder: When nature uses the word "energy" in relationship to form, it means that what we normally cannot perceive through our sensory system is energy. What we can see, feel, taste, etc., is form.

And this is what nature can give you now. It understands the relationship of energy to form and it knows what is required in order for spirit and the soul's direction and purpose to perfectly seat into form in balance. As we have pointed out a number of times, nature is the master of involution and the expert in matters involving the relationship of energy to form. In order to create support systems that respond to this new demand of human souls seeking to ground a broader picture of reality into form, man must turn to nature.

We do not mean to imply that if man turns to nature for the needed development of his support systems that this development will be effortless and perceived as perfect. We have no intention of perpetuating a parent/child dynamic in our relationship with mankind. We have no intention of dictating structure and process. In fact, this would be impossible. Humans must supply intent, purpose, direction and need when it *comes to systems development. With this definition, we in nature will seek to supply the best structure in which to accommodate and move intent, purpose, direction and need. It is a true partnership we seek. We will not interfere with or attempt to alter the human evolutionary thrust. We are here to assist and accommodate this thrust.*

In medicine, humans have seen the relationship of nature to themselves in the areas of nutrition, natural medicines and stress relief. Humans do not see themselves as nature/human soul systems requiring involution/evolution balance. Instead, they see themselves as souls utilizing nature in form for the purpose of evolutionary growth. Nature has been the servant of the soul while the primary thrust of the human has been evolutionary. This cannot and does not work. The human system itself is a partnership between soul and nature, and its thrust, its primary focus, is the involution/evolution balance. When in form, and we mean by this any existence within the band of form, the human must strive for involution/evolution balance in order to achieve evolutionary movement. Without this balance, there is no evolutionary movement, activation or change. The involution dynamic is the tool of the movement, activation and changes required by the evolution dynamic.

THE ARENA OF
EMOTIONAL/MENTAL HEALTH

First of all, let us say that we refer to this arena as "emotional/mental" because the dynamics causing a person to be classified in need of emotional or mental assistance are, from nature's perspective, the same. The distinction between the two is created by humans and does not concern nature.

You will recall, Machaelle, from your personal exploration in this area that when you came upon an emotional block that seemed impossible for you to get through, you asked us in nature for help. We will say now that the insight to ask for help was, in fact, initiated from us of nature and in response to our desire to assist you in any way possible. You picked up on this insight and acted on it by opening with the intent for us to assist you. It is essential that people understand that in areas where nature links with the human soul, it (nature) can only do so on request. We do not assume a partnership. To do so would be to override human free will and thus render the soul powerless. This would be against universal law, and nature, on its own, does not live or function outside universal law.

As you told us what your emotional situation was, we observed the energy dynamics as they shifted and moved throughout your system on all PEMS levels. (We see the human system on all PEMS levels because that complete system is functioning in a form state.) We were able to observe the emotional blocks you were struggling with from the perspective of energy. From these observations, we were able to alter the blocks as well as the general movement of energy in a way that assisted and made more efficient that energy's movement. In short, we assisted you in achieving involution/evolution balance in those areas where you had temporarily lost it. As a result, you experienced the shifts, insights, releases and understanding required in the re-establishing of involution/evolution balance throughout your entire system. Remember, we see these blocks from the standpoint of energy—what is moving appropriately and what is not. We see your system as energy relating to form from the perspective of involution/evolution balance. We do not define what results in insights, understanding and resolution. This is the evolutionary input and thrust for which **you** are responsible.

Our process with you is an example both of the partnership we seek with humans and how we can work together in every way to achieve full, inspirited, functioning form. Where the will of the human is present, and where we of nature have been requested to help, we will adjust, shift and facilitate the involution systems in order to support the human's evolution process. For us, it is a relatively simple matter to work with you in this way. In fact, it is solely a matter of receiving a person's request for our assistance.

We suggest that we work together using the following process.

CALIBRATION PROCESS STEPS

1. Open a Healing Coning: Deva of Healing, Pan, a link with the White Brotherhood, your higher self.

NOTE: We recommend that flower essences be used in this process. We suggest that the person test for essences after opening the coning and prior to stating the problem. This will stabilize the person throughout the *process. A dosage need not be tested for, since any essences needed in the beginning of the process will be for short-term stabilization.*

2. Request assistance with a problem that is primarily focused on the emotional or mental levels.

3. State the problem. State it as if you were telling a therapist. Talk about the problem itself and how it is affecting you physically, emotionally, mentally and/or spiritually.

4. Once you have given a full description, allow yourself a half-hour to move through the insight, release, understanding and resolution stages.

NOTE: *You may not perceive any changes in attitude or understanding during the half-hour. This will be because the process of shifting understanding and changes in attitude sometimes needs to move through more complex levels in order to reach a point where one can perceive the effects. We suggest that if you have sat quietly for a half-hour and no sense of understanding or resolution has come to you, simply move forward in faith that very shortly, within twenty-four hours, you will experience understanding, change and resolution.*

5. We suggest that you test for flower essences again just prior to closing the coning and include a dosage/solution test for continued support during the integration process.

6. Close the coning by asking to be disconnected from each member of the coning, one at a time. Test, using kinesiology, to make sure the coning is closed. (If you test negative after asking if it is closed, just refocus on the coning and again request to be disconnected from each member, one at a time. You simply lost your focus the first time. After the second time, you will test positive.)

ADDITIONAL NOTES: *We see some emotional/mental problems as comparatively complex layerings of energy movement. It is quite possible that for the **final** resolution of an emotional/mental issue, one will need to go through this process several times. But we also stress that timing is a key factor. If and when a follow-up session is needed, you will sense something related to the original problem that has become an issue. One need not plan ahead for these follow-ups, for you will need time between sessions to* *integrate the insight, release, understanding and resolution from the previous session.*

*The half-hour timing more than covers the time span we need to move the human system through involution/evolution imbalance into involution/evolution balance. Don't forget that in the more complex situations, you will be moving through a **series** of sessions with us that will resemble the peeling process or two-week process described in the book, Flower Essences. You will move through one layer at a time, experiencing a sense of resolution after each layer, which, once integrated, will signal you to move on to the next layer.*

For a twenty-four hour period of time after a calibration, you may feel tired and a little quiet—even feel an ache or pain that has seemingly popped up from nowhere. These are simply reactions to the calibration and should be gone within twenty-four hours. The integration-period flower essences solution will assist and stabilize you greatly through this twenty-four hour period. However, if a reaction should persist, set up another Calibration Process around the same issue and explain all of the various reactions you are having. Nature will do additional adjustments that will either move you through or eliminate the reactions.

The Calibration Process is an additional nature-partnership procedure that is not in and of itself strictly a flower essence process. With or without the essences, this process can work. Flower essences would be most helpful, however, in stabilizing you throughout the Calibration Process itself and afterwards during the time needed for integrating the work accomplished during the process.

CALIBRATION PROCESS FOR THE GARDEN

Not long after I began using the process for myself, nature modified it for use in the garden. There will be times when the garden environment or some specific element of the garden (plant, insect, soil . . .) will receive an ecological impact that will be so strong that the form and the devic dynamic within that form will no longer be synchronized. Soil balancing and triangle balancing will not address this specific situation. The Calibration Process will, and the process is simple.

1. Open a 4-point coning, including the deva of whatever you are working with. Balance and stabilize the coning. Test yourself for flower essences.

2. Ask:
     Is a Calibration Process needed here? (Test)
If no, see "Troubleshooting," (chapter 11) for how to proceed.

3. If yes, ask:
     Is the process to be done by itself or in conjunction with the Troubleshooting Process?
This is an either/or question, and you will test its parts: Process to be done alone? (Test) Process to be done in conjunction with the Troubleshooting Process? (Test)

If it is to be done in conjunction with the Troubleshooting Process, read the Troubleshooting section before continuing on. If it is to be done alone, continue on now.

4. Ask Pan for assistance. (Pan is already in the coning, but you will need to "alert" Pan of your intention to initiate the Calibration Process.)

5. State:
     I ask that this form be synchronized with its devic dynamic, and I ask, with Pan's assistance, that this be done now.

6. Wait quietly for 30 seconds for the calibration to occur. After 30 seconds, verify that the process is complete. If you get a no, wait another 15 seconds and verify again. This time you will get a yes.

7. Test for balancer needs (soil balancing kit). Shift the balancers exactly as you normally would with Pan for the Soil Balancing and Stabilizing Process.

8. Test for stabilizer needs (flower essences). Shift the essences with Pan.

9. The process is over. Close the coning. Verify. And test yourself for essences and a dosage.

CALIBRATION PROCESS

Use the soil balancing kit and flower essences.

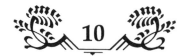

10

Using the
Energy Processes

By now, you have asked yourself at least a hundred times, "How do I know when to use these energy processes?" At least with the environmental processes in the *Workbook*, you had a sequential progression that moved you from the first process of establishing a partnership with nature to the last process of discovering late-season succession planting rhythms. The energy processes are used during the garden planning, planting time and seasonal maintenance time.

Here are some hints:

WHEN TO USE THE PROCESSES

1. Each year, before you do any garden planning, test a list of the energy processes and find out which ones, if any, need to be done *before* you begin the *Workbook's* environmental processes. If you are to do several processes, test to find out the order in which they are to be done. ("Is _____ Process first?" Test.)

Then find out *when* you are to do the *first* process. Allow nature to create the pattern of the energy processes for you. Your testing will be as follows:

Do I do this process in January? (Test)

February? (Test)

March? (Test)

Whichever month tests positive, that's the one. Then test for which week.

Do I do the process the first week? (Test)

Second week? (Test)

Third week? (Test)

Whichever week tests positive, that's the week. Now you have the month and week. To be even more precise, test which day of that week would be best to do the process. Obviously, if you have something scheduled for a specific day that you cannot change, that day is not available for you to do the process—so tell nature your schedule and don't test for the process on that day.

You now have the order in which you are to do the "pre-season" energy processes, but I suggest you not do a timing schedule for the list of processes all at one time. After doing the first process, ask if you are to do the second process immediately. If so, you will stay in the coning, shift your focus to the second process, adjust the coning accordingly for the second process and proceed.

If you were not to do them back to back, wait twenty-four hours after completing the first process, and then find out when you are to do the second process. The twenty-four-hour period allows nature time to see the response to the first process, and it will schedule the next process in light of the response. In this way, you will be working with nature with more agility and flexibility.

Very likely, there will be some energy processes that will be scheduled during the time you are doing all of the garden planning and planting. Just let the energy-processes timetable interweave as you do the environmental processes and move into the planting cycle.

2. Once the garden is planted, you are in the garden maintenance period that I call "phase 3." Phase 1 is the planning and chart work. Phase 2 is the planting period. Phase 3 is maintenance and harvesting. And phase 4 is putting the garden to bed.

During phase 3, I hold weekly "meetings" with nature to find out what I am to do that will maintain and support the garden patterns and rhythms throughout the growing season. This meeting idea is a refinement since I wrote the *Workbook,* and I highly recommend it to you. *I* need to do the meeting weekly in order to keep up with the experiments that are going on in the Perelandra garden. You may only need to do the meetings every two weeks or every three weeks. I suggest that you get this timing from nature. ("How often do I need to meet with you in order to maintain the garden's balance and growth cycle? Every week?" [Test] "Every two weeks?" [Test] And so on, until you test positive.)

For the meeting, you will need your garden chart, your triangle identification chart, a list of environmental needs (watering, fertilizing, thinning, etc.) and energy processes, pencil/pen and paper—and a cup of coffee. You do not need to be in the garden for the meeting. (You may wish to be in the garden when doing the energy processes because this may give you a more immediate feeling as you are working with specific areas and plants, but this is not necessary. As long as you can hold your focus on what you are doing, you can do the processes from your house. Do what you need to do that will help you to comfortably maintain focus.)

GARDEN MEETING PROCESS

1. Open a 4-point coning. Include the deva of your garden if it is not already in the coning. Balance and stabilize the coning, and test yourself for essences.

2. State that you wish to have the scheduled garden meeting.

3. Move through the garden chart section by section and/or row by row, asking for each planting in the row:
Does _____ need anything? (Test)
If you get a positive, test your list of environmental needs: watering, weeding, cultivating, root fertilizing, foliar feeding, thinning, more sun, less sun, pruning, harvesting . . . The last thing on your list will be "troubleshooting." Whatever tests positive, that is what you are to do. If you tested positive for "troubleshooting," make a

note of what plant(s) need it and hold this off until the end of the garden meeting.

Keep notes on which plants need what and how much. If you need to fertilize, find out what you are to fertilize with and how much you are to use. If you are to thin, find out proportionally, how much you are to thin. If you are to water, find out how many quarts or gallons per plant, or how many watering cans per section. *Don't assume anything. As with the early planning stages, ask nature everything.* This is where we learn how differently nature would like us to approach garden maintenance.

HINT: I have made a chart for the Perelandra garden and divided it into sections and rows within each section, so that I can keep tabs on who needs what in which row. I find it to be an efficient way to keep track of all this information.

4. When you have completed testing of all the various vegetables, herbs and flowers (and whatever else you felt should be tested), turn your focus to the triangle identification chart. Move through this chart as you did the garden chart—section by section and/or row by row. For whatever vegetable, herb or flower is triangulated, ask:

Does this triangle need balancing and stabilizing? (Test)

Whatever tests positive, ascertain which point(s) or link(s) are weak and in need of help. Then balance and stabilize each weak point and/or link using the regular Plant Triangulation Process.

Don't panic on this. Again, once you have done your initial triangle balancing in the spring, you will need to do it again only occasionally. During the entire growing season this year, I have had to do the triangle balance once. Making the garden-triangle check a part of the weekly meetings both assures me that all of the triangle points and links are balanced and strong and tells me when a triangle weakens. By doing the balancing and stabilizing right away, I can stop a weakened triangle condition from irrevocably damaging its plant points.

5. Ask if there is anything else you may need to know that hasn't been covered. If you get a yes, and it doesn't come to you right away, just state:

Give me a hint as to what it is.

Whatever pops into mind first is the hint. You can verify this by testing. ("Is this what you mean?" Test.)

Then add it to your list of things to do.

6. The meeting is now finished. Thank your team, close the coning and check yourself for essences and dosage.

If anything tested positive for troubleshooting, you can keep the coning activated and continue right on with the Troubleshooting Process. (See chapter 11.)

HINT: Whatever the meeting rhythm is for you, whether it be weekly or every two weeks or whatever, I have found that nature prefers that we hold to this rhythm. That is, we meet with them on the day that we have agreed to meet and not arbitrarily change the schedule. If you cannot hold a meeting on one of the days, connect with Pan and tell him that you won't be able to meet. Then let him know when you can hold that meeting. Any necessary patterns and rhythms will be adjusted accordingly. So when you are working out your meeting schedule with nature, give some thought to what day of the week you are most often free enough to have the meeting.

At first glance, this may appear awfully tedious and an invitation to nature to *never* let you out of the garden. But I have been doing these meetings for several seasons now and I am amazed at the light touch a co-creative garden needs throughout the growing cycle. What the weekly meeting does for me is take the guesswork out of moving a garden through the summer and early fall months. It actually *frees* up my time considerably, and I don't waste time wondering if I should be doing something in the garden. It also changes how we *think* we should tend a garden during this time. Just as the *Workbook* processes break down all the preconceived and traditional notions about garden planning and development, the garden meetings do the same for garden maintenance. The meetings give nature the communication structure it needs for continuing its work with us during these months.

I'm including portions of several meetings I've had, particularly the session for setting up the meeting process and the first meeting, so that you can see the kinds of information I get from them and the issues I might bring up in a meeting. I do a regular session translation for most of my meetings. You will be working more with the question/answer format and kinesiology.

NATURE SESSION
Nature Coning—5 June 1988
Opening the Phase 3 Weekly Meeting Process

We are aware of the purpose for this meeting and have looked forward to it for some months now. As you have intuitively felt, it is time to develop the next stage. You have called this stage "phase 3" and we will concur with you on this name. Whenever we wish to work within this stage with you, we will identify it by the name "phase 3."

Your sense that phase 3 relates to the continued unfolding of a co-creative garden once the initial plans have been completed in form in the garden is essentially correct. Just as there was timing, patterning and rhythm reflected in the planting plans, there is a continuation of this as the plans unfold and mature in form. There is harmonic relationship maintained between what was begun with planting and what continues during the growth and maturation process.

The unusual shift that the Perelandra garden took in mid-season last year directly relates to what we now identify as phase 3. This shift was in preparation for a new level of conscious operation in the garden which, in part, has been what was heralded in when you dedicated the garden, Perelandra and yourself to the next step this spring.

Up to this point in the Perelandra development, you have faithfully and skillfully executed our plans and patterns into form. Once initiated, the clarity of your action and its translation of the original devic plans have served to move the garden in balance through its growth and maturation process.

The garden and Perelandra as a whole have broadened their scope and service. This requires that phase 3 be instituted in order to move the garden, you and Perelandra in tandem with the new scope of intent and purpose. Conscious action is far more desirable than unconscious action. Consequently, you will now become a conscious partner with us during the time period referred to as "phase 3." Phase 3 will continue until the final "putting-to-bed" process. As with phase 3, you then will enter a new phase (phase 4, if you will) that, although different, will be harmoniously related to phases 1, 2 and 3. We suggest that to cap this new and exciting year, you continue the process you are about to begin throughout phase 4, as well. At that point, the symphony that was initiated devically when you called in the next phase during last fall's equinox, and has moved through its various movements, focused on translating the devic plan from one level to another: phase 2, translating the plan to form; phase 3, maintaining harmonious patterning throughout growth and maturation; and phase 4, releasing the energy of natural balance back into the universe—all of these will complete the symphony in its broadest, deepest orchestration.

We suggest on a practical level for phase 3 that you meet with us weekly and that, whenever possible, the rhythm of the weekly meetings be maintained so that we can project ahead within a specific and short (7 days) time frame and give you information pertaining to the garden and Perelandra. We further suggest that you not choose Sunday, since this will be the day following the workshops and you should not press yourself so quickly into a nature session. If at any time you see that one weekly rhythm is not conveniently working out for you, go ahead and change to a new pattern—but let us know a week ahead of the change so that we can adjust our information accordingly.

I think you will be pleasantly surprised at the small amount of information, relatively speaking, of course, requiring action on your part. You will not be run ragged, let us assure you. Small touches will be made from time to time. This will be included with the usual garden maintenance process that you have been doing already, but which will now be done in a stronger, clearer response to rhythm.

Also, throughout these weekly sessions we will be adding to your personal knowledge about nature, form and their relationship to energy and, ultimately, the whole. We say this to you so that you will open the meeting prepared for a computer session.

*We have picked up on your questions about the effects of ultraviolet rays (regarding the destruction of the ozone layer) and their effects on you. In short, should you take special precautions in light of your work outdoors and the fact that you have a personal family history that includes many cases of cancer. To be brief, you do **not** need to take any special precaution* *beyond that which you are taking. We suggest that you not work during the hot afternoon hours, but this is because it is not harmonious to you or the garden to be working yourself and plants during the intensity of the afternoon sun. We counsel you to continue using your common sense and to pattern your approach to outdoor work based on the effect on you of the hot sun and other weather factors. Ultraviolet rays need not be of any concern to you if you'll continue with your present level of common sense.*

Another point, one which you've sensed already: Just as the Perelandra environment excludes from it aspects of surrounding environments that are not harmonious with the Perelandra balance, it also excludes any level of ultraviolet rays that would be inappropriate to the Perelandra balance. This balance is strong and vibrant and, as such, responds to the planetary environment in strong and vibrant ways. Its strength includes that which is appropriate and further enhances the harmony and balance, and it excludes that which is not appropriate. The Perelandra balance cannot be achieved and maintained on one level and with one collection of "aspects" without shifting and changing all corresponding levels and all aspects which they enfold.

For now, we suggest that, unless you have any questions, this session be closed. The next session will begin the phase 3 process and rhythm.

Machaelle: How about Tuesdays?

Coning: That is perfectly fine with us.

Machaelle: See you this Tuesday then. Is there anything I should or could do in the garden before Tuesday?

Coning: We suggest nothing. Allow the garden to settle into the completion of phase 2 for a couple of days. By the way, the translation of devic patterning to the charts and into form was especially strong this year and serves as a fine foundation for this new development. Spend tomorrow relaxing and observing. (Close coning.)

NATURE SESSION
Garden Coning—7 June 1988
First Weekly Phase 3 Garden Session

Since phase 3 has already been set up in the last session regarding intent and process, we will get right to the business of implementing phase 3 into the garden timing.

Phase 2, the translation, as you call it, of the devic garden plans into the form reality of the garden, is now complete. The quality of this translation, the precision of your work, has been especially keen this year and has gone a long way in launching this new area of our partnership. As you will see, what you have accomplished so far will directly relate to the timing and amount of adjustments, shifts and growth-promoting work that you will do between now and phase 4. So, if you wish to go through the garden chart, row by row and area by area, we can give you the information needed for the garden area for next week. If any questions should come up for you, please do not hesitate to insert the questions where they arise as we move through the garden chart.

Machaelle: Should I begin with the garden center or the garden outer ring?

Coning: Begin with the outer rings and work towards the very center of the garden. This is so that when you get to the point of the most concentrated power, the rest of the garden will be fully shifted and capable of "handling" any change that might occur in the center. Although the center is the power plant of this garden, it is also the touch-down point for all that is beyond the garden that is related to or a part of the workings of the garden and the Perelandra process in general. To maintain balance, the garden proper must have its changes and shifts activated on the level of intent prior to any changes pertaining to the activity related to the garden's center. To reverse the process and to work with the center prior to addressing the garden proper would throw the rest of the garden and the larger garden area into a state of "catch-up."

Machaelle: Should I make it a practice to institute the phase 3 changes and to work the garden in general starting with the outer rings and moving to the center?

Coning: We need to address this question according to the phase in which you are working. Phase 3 should have its information translated into the garden's outer rings, and then work towards the center. Phases 1, 2 and 4 should have the focus beginning in the center, and then work towards the outer ring. In order to not tire you, let's address the whys for this question at a later date. For now, it is important to know in which direction you'll be working. As the summer progresses, you will see that there will be times when these sessions concentrate more on insight rather than action.

Machaelle: Let's go through the chart then. Any specific section we should start with?

Coning: Any one you wish. You've been starting with the Blueberry Section throughout all the previous chart information and you may wish to be consistent with this.

Blueberry Section

The Perelandra garden is 100 feet in diameter. It is divided into 3 sections, each section containing 1/3 of the circular rows. Rows 1 through 7 are where the annual vegetable, herbs and flowers are planted. The outer ring, consisting of 4 rows, is actually a perennial band containing the roses plus a different perennial in each section: blueberry bushes in the Blueberry Section, raspberries and asparagus in the Raspberry/Asparagus Section and strawberries in the Strawberry Section. (Now you know where I got the clever names for the sections.)

Outer Ring

Coning: Roses: Kelp. Per plant, add 3/4 c (cup).

Machaelle: Any changes in the mulch?

Coning: No. Just work the kelp through the mulch so that it will be available to the roots.

Machaelle: Will this help the black spot I've noticed?

Coning: Yes, but the black spot is still a part of the rose ring because the final balance has not yet been put into place. The rose-ring balance of which we speak has to do specifically with the ring around the Perelandra garden as well as the overall balance and relationship of the rose genus to the planet. Continuing through the patient growth and balance process in the Perelandra garden will net exceptional healing and balancing within the rose family and its relationship to the planet. The rose balance will move in stages, and the Perelandra rose ring is exactly where it should be in light of the balance of the garden, the intent of Perelandra and the overall balance of the planet as it moves through transition. Just keep moving through the process as we suggest, and in the timing we suggest and all of this will be accomplished. Every time a shift occurs in the Perelandra rose ring, we must observe the shift in relationship to the garden and to the whole. Every time a major shift occurs within the planet's transition, it must be translated in kind to the Perelandra rose ring. It is not by chance that the Perelandra garden is encircled by roses. You know this. If you wish to see the effects of the rose ring in tangible ways, watch the people who come to the garden. Watch how some will experience the garden from outside the rose ring and others will enter the garden's heart space and experience it from inside. You can see the rose ring as the "skin" of the garden, which must adjust to the dynamics both from within the garden and outside. In short, for your understanding, it is important not to rush the timing and development of the rose-ring balance, for its life-giving energy must remain in balance with the internal and in relationship to the outside.

Machaelle: Gotcha. Is there anything else I should do for these roses this week?

Coning: No. Except, if you see any more damaged canes, go ahead and remove them.

Machaelle: OK.

Coning: Blueberries: Nothing need be done for the present. They're doing quite nicely.

Row 7:

Wax Beans: Cover the row lightly with some straw. You need not wait for rain.

Machaelle: Do we have the correct white onion set interplanting ratio?

Coning: Yes. This is good. Planting the sets throughout the row was a strong move in terms of energy.

Yellow and Red Onions: Nothing need be done now. The interplanting ratio is good. If you wish to move straw into the row now, that will be fine. There is no hurry on this, however.

Watermelon: Row OK. Don't cover with hay yet.

Row 6:

Broccoli: Surround plants with mulch now. Don't make it more than an inch deep, however. The interplanting ratio is fine.

Mustard Greens: Thin again and pull no more than an inch of mulch around the plants.

Row 5:

Red Petunias: Both sides: Mulch lightly. But don't crowd the plants. Mulch the open soil around them.

Lettuces: Thin again and bring mulch in closer to the row. Don't crowd though. This won't be the final mulching, if another is needed. (We realize that was contradictory; however, we simply don't want you to approach this mulching as if it was the final bedding in for the season.)

Row 4:

Green Bean I: You can start harvesting whatever radishes you wish for eating and sharing. You need not approach this harvesting as if it were for the purpose of removing the radishes from the row. Approach the harvesting with the intent of sharing the radishes with a few friends (if you wish) and of leaving some radishes in the row. Don't worry about the radishes that are ready for harvesting being left in the row. They're part of the row energy component. Bring the mulch in closer to the row where necessary. This will lower the "mulch wall" and allow the row to spread wide.

Row 3:

Green Cabbage: Thin to one plant per cabbage "hill." Don't pull the mulch in around the plants yet.

Machaelle: Is the petunia ratio correct in light of the pink color not being especially soft?

Coning: The ratio is fine. Although not the softest, this color is most acceptable and does the balancing job well. Your efforts in attempting to locate the softest pink are appreciated.

Row 2:

Zucchini I: Nothing needed yet.
Yellow Squash I: Thin lightly.

Row 1:

Golden Peppers: Mulch lightly. Water each plant before mulching.
Green Peppers: Mulch lightly and water before mulching.
Yellow Marigolds: Don't mulch yet.

Raspberry/Asparagus Section

Outer Ring

Roses: Kelp. Per bush, add 2/3 c. Work into mulch.
Berries: The canes are fine. If you wish to thin the canes that have come up outside the rope area, that may be done this week.

Asparagus: Bone meal: per band width x 3', add 2-1/3 c. Kelp: (same space), add 1 c. Lightly work the fertilizers through the mulch. Don't add additional mulch this week. Allow rain to make the fertilizers available to the soil and root systems before putting on the season's straw.

Row 7:

Okra: Thin lightly. Parsley OK.

White Zinnia: If sets of true leaves appear on the seedlings by the end of the week, thin lightly. Otherwise, the plants and seedlings are fine.

Brussels Sprouts: You jumped the gun a little on this. The second thinning was fine. Don't pull mulch in yet.

Celery: Thin down to one plant per clump. Mulch lightly on both sides of the row.

Row 6:

Yellow and Red Onions: Mulch lightly.

Green Bean II: Cover row with mulch until planting time.

Row 5:

Snap Peas: Fine. You can mulch lightly around the onions and in front of the row.

Cantaloupe: Okay.

Row 4:

Fennel and Red Basil: Thin down to one plant for each clump, except for the double red basil. Mulch around the plants lightly. Also, prune the red basil's spent flowers.

Row 3:

Beets: The thinning was fine. No need to mulch yet. You may mulch lightly around the onion plants, however, reducing the mulch wall against which they are butted.

Row 2:

Yellow and Red Onions: Mulch lightly.

Spinach: Mulch lightly. This will spur the growth. The spinach is actually doing well in its balancing role in the garden. If you wish, more can be planted at the end of the season for fall harvesting.

Row 1:

Red Cabbage: *Don't mulch yet. Plants and petunias are fine as is.*
Marigolds: *Mulch lightly.*

Strawberry Section

Outer Ring

Roses: *Per bush, add 3/4 c kelp. Work through the mulch.*
Strawberries: *Enjoy! Anytime you wish to add the pine mulch where you ran out this spring is fine. Don't remove the nightshade yet. This and the sorrel are actually a part of the balance of the garden and of the strawberry row in particular. How the plants weave in and out with the growth cycle of the strawberries is important.*

Row 7:

Corn: *Cover row, if you wish.*
Cauliflower: *Begin new plants in flats for summer planting. The timing on the cauliflower has shifted. Mulch the row and the existing onion plants. The interplanting intent of the onions is just fine and can hold down the row well until it is time to transplant the cauliflower into the row.*
Burgundy Petunias: *Water with fish emulsion solution to stimulate the root systems. Per gal. water, add 4-1/2 Tbl. fish emulsion concentrate.*
Yellow and Red Onions: *Mulch lightly.*

Row 6:

Corn: *Close row, if you wish.*
Onions: *Mulch lightly.*
Kale: *Thin again, and bring the mulch closer into (but not around) the plants.*

Row 5:

Garlic: *Mulch.*
Limas: *Where needed, bring mulch in closer to the row.*

Row 4:

Coral Petunias: *Lightly mulch around plants without crowding.*
Golden Melons: *Fine.*

Row 3:

> *Carrots: Thinning was fine. Bring mulch in closer to the row. No need to water prior.*
>
> *White Onion Sets: Mulch medium.*

Row 2:

> *Dill: Reduce to one plant per clump. Mulch lightly.*
>
> *Salvia: Mulch lightly after watering.*

Row 1:

> *Jalapeno Peppers: Mulch lightly.*
>
> *Anaheim Peppers: Mulch lightly. No need to water either prior to mulching.*
>
> *Marigolds: Mulch lightly.*

Garden Center

> *Annual Ring: Fine.*
>
> *Herb Ring: Nothing Needed.*
>
> *Mineral Ring: Fine.*
>
> *Center: Fine.*

Garden Area:

> *Nothing needed. This is now stabilized for the season, thanks to the work you did with the meadow, wildflowers and grass. Also, the area around the cabin (a part of the garden area) is stabilized well and needs only to be moved through the growth process as perceived visually. The various annuals you have included would benefit from foliar feeding about every 3 weeks throughout the season. You may begin that cycle this week. This includes the container annuals as well as the bedding annuals.*

Flower Triangles:

> *They are to be treated as you treat the annual flowers around the cabin. They would benefit from foliar feeding, like the other annuals, every three weeks. During the heat of the summer, the triangle annuals, as well as the cabin annuals, may be watered. Annuals have a shallow root system and, without heavy mulching, sometimes suffer more than is necessary or desirable during the high heat of the summer. Let your observation give you the needed*

The rest of the 1988 phase 3 meetings continued the rhythms that were initiated in this first meeting. Some weeks, I was able to finish the garden chores in a half hour. There were even weeks where I had nothing to do. Other weeks, I had 2 or 3 hours worth of work. But throughout, I felt the precision and purpose in every move I made. And I never felt I was guessing about what needed to be done. This freed me up mentally and emotionally—and time-wise.

input for this. If ever there is a question about watering needs, consult the nature spirits attending the specific areas.

This firmly launches you and the garden (and us, we might add) into phase 3. You need not concern yourself with specific days for doing the various jobs needed. From time to time, we will recommend specific days within a week for specific jobs, but this will be more the exception than the rule. We are assuming the weekly period to begin on Tuesdays and to end the following Monday evening.

Machaelle: I think that about covers it. I'll just concentrate on what you have recommended and not worry about anything else.

Coning: That immediate focus will be exactly what is called for as we move through this process. Observe and enjoy the differences in the garden this year as we move it through this new level of phase 3. (Phase 3 has, of course, always been a part of the Perelandra garden cycle. This year it is opening on a new level. Don't think that the phase itself has not been a part of the garden until now, or that your care-tending up to now has been out of step or not really important. The opposite is the truth of the matter. And now it is time for what has been to move to the next level.

Machaelle: Unless I have any questions, I'll see you next week.

Coning: Good. (Close coning.)

The following year, 1989, we had over twenty-five inches of rainfall from May 1 to August 1. I had never dealt with flooding and monsoons before. Consequently, I opened a special meeting during phase 2 to get input on what was happening in the garden and how I was to proceed.

NATURE SESSION
Garden Coning—16 May 1989
Re: Recent heavy rains and garden rhythm

Good afternoon. We are pleased that you opened this session for clarification on the garden planting rhythm in light of the recent period of rain you are experiencing. We have sensed your concern and wish to take this time to alleviate any feelings of concern or even defeat you might have.

As you already know, the original planting rhythms that were given to you in late winter had built in an accommodation for a cold, wet spring. The planting has been scheduled in what appears to be a later rhythm. In fact, the rhythm has not been late at all. Lateness, as far as nature is concerned, is not measured by the days on the calendar but rather by a combination of natural conditions. Simply by considering the combination of moisture, soil temperature and air temperature throughout these spring weeks, it is easy to see that a planting rhythm that is just now beginning to gear up in earnest is not late. We realize that this is something you intuitively understand through both common sense and observing the relationship between the annual planting rhythm and the spring weather over the years. We simply wished to bring forward this information now in order that we may build on top of it as we answer the concerns about this year's rhythm and weather.

Of course this spring is unusual in the amount of rainfall your area has experienced. However, when nature rhythms are viewed in the long term, such a spring is not at all unusual. Periodically there are droughts and, at other times, there are heavy, extended rain periods. All of this is part of the natural relief and balancing system contained within nature. Humans tend to desire a natural rhythm that is consistently repeated annually so that certain conditions can be depended on and planned for. As you know, such a thing does not exist except in the wishful thinking of humans.

The key, of course, to working with natural conditions is flexibility. Built within the survival patterns of all species within all of the kingdoms of nature is a strong pattern of flexibility. This is essential, as you can imagine. For humans to successfully join the dance within nature, they must approach nature and work with the intent of flexibility. Otherwise, as nature bends to respond to the moment, man will be left standing in the elements, like a ramrod, static and, consequently, vulnerable to the moment.

If the relationship between man and nature could be left at this point, there would not be a problem as far as nature is concerned. Nature would simply bend, endure and continue its journey through life. However, right at the moment when nature is practicing flexibility and man is inflexible, he turns to nature, takes on a dominant role and attempts to force nature into his inflexible stance. This is a most unnatural position for nature to be in. Often nature is able to become even more flexible for the sake of surviving the threatening input of man at this point, but sometimes the kingdoms of nature being affected are weakened by the additional burden and are ultimately destroyed.

To return to the question of the annual planting rhythm: The pattern for the cold, wet spring was taken into consideration this winter, as we have said. The pattern was in place on every level. Now, when such a pattern is formed, it is activated and released within the Earth's atmosphere for its playing out in form. Just as with everything else within both nature and the human element, once patterns and spirit are released within the level of form, they become a part of the whole that is playing out around it in form. The pattern then adjusts appropriately to the larger picture. It does not remain an isolated pattern seeking to play out in a form reality in complete disregard to that which exists around it.

When this spring's weather pattern moved into form, it adjusted accordingly to the whole. Consequently, there is no such thing as "precise" weather patterns where the exact location and exact measurement of rainfall could be predicted. We on the devic level can only create the appropriate patterns and release them into life's pattern. The nature spirits can only work to fuse these patterns into the whole fabric of form as it exists at the present time—they cannot indulge in wishful thinking in a desire to have "perfect" conditions upon which to play out these patterns. This would be unnatural on all levels. The patterns are released and they are fused into whatever exists at that moment.

There was a time on the Earth level when prediction regarding weather patterns and natural cycles could be made from the intelligences of nature with what was considered accuracy. This is because the interrelationship between nature and the humans on the Earth level had not reached the critical state in which it is now. Man's attempts to dominate nature regarding its natural rhythms and its responses to natural rhythms were, in comparison to today, slight. The environment in which patterns were released was still dominated by nature. A rain pattern could be predicted with continued accuracy from creation of that pattern to physical fruition. Now, with the many souls inhabiting the Earth plane, the balance has tipped and the environment is more human-dominant. That is, the natural patterns and rhythms playing out in form within the Earth plane are having to respond and adjust to man's willful intent of how he thinks his environment should be.

We return to flexibility for, as we have said, it is flexibility that is the key now to working with nature during what look to be disastrous times and during those times when the simple annual patterns are seeking to unfold.

You have the planting rhythm for the Perelandra garden as it was originally perceived in late winter. Since then, the weather patterns have come into form. Nature is not static—ever. Therefore, it would be folly for nature to expect the original planting plan to remain rigidly in effect. The basic tone of the planting rhythms will remain, but the plan itself will require fine-tuning.

As you move through the remaining planting rhythm, check with us (either on the devic level or the nature spirit level) for adjustments to the rhythm. We would prefer that these adjustments be done in the moment; i.e., as you are preparing for the next planting, find out if there have been any changes. You already know that this week's planting has been changed—in essence, cut in half. And that an extra planting day has been added to accommodate this change next week. You will also note that although this week's planting has been changed, it is still scheduled to be completed before the May 28th planting. So the intent of the original rhythm has been maintained. We suggest that as you plan for the May 28th planting, you find out what changes have been made. That day, as of now, will also be divided into at least two more days.

One other thing you have noted: This week's above-ground planting has been divided and rescheduled on days in which the moon cycle is best for root-crop planting. Again notice the flexibility while maintaining intent. Although that which is being planted is not a "root crop," it is still a planting of crops in general. So the root-crop cycle of the moon is being utilized to add the greater flexibility.

In general, let us say that the garden at Perelandra is very much on target, as is the entire activity at Perelandra. The garden will move very quickly once out of the rain cycle. In fact, it will be at a speed that will astound you, because the plant life-cycle will be moving unimpeded as a result of the individual soil balancing work you are doing. If you have any specific questions, we can answer them now.

Machaelle: The lettuce seeds are under 3 inches of water. Should I plan for replanting?

Coning: No. They will be fine. You planted the seeds thickly, and plenty are ready for germination. Your sense to dig a small ditch on either side of the row will be helpful in draining the water from the seeds in the low-lying part of the row. But that shouldn't be done until tomorrow. The seeds are simply "waiting" for the conditions that would support germination. The eleven days of rain have placed germination on hold (an example of nature's flexibility) but it has not been long enough or hard enough to destroy the seeds' chance for germination.

Machaelle: I'm scheduled for spreading straw now. I'm assuming that this timing has been rescheduled also.

Coning: Yes. We suggest waiting a couple of weeks—till the end of May.

Machaelle: I think I have a good sense of how to move through the rest of the spring planting cycle. In essence, I'll just stick close to you and let you lead me through it—while keeping records of the changes, of course.

Coning: The records will be helpful to those who come along behind you and need verification as to the success of flexibility. You will see many who will seek to form a partnership with us but who will do so by placing themselves in a subservient role while placing nature in an inflexible role. Whatever is suggested from our level will become carved in stone, as they say, never to be modified. So evidence of the flexible relationship that has gone on here at Perelandra will be most helpful to them.

Machaelle: For now, I have no more questions. If it's agreed, I'll close the coning.

Coning: We have completed what we wished to communicate to you for now and are pleased to have this time together in this fashion.

Machaelle: Same here. Thank you.

Coning: You are most welcome. (Close coning.)

I moved through the early summer with nature and, for the most part, I was amazed at what was occurring in the garden. But as the annual September Open House closed in, I became concerned about how this garden looked. In early August, it looked like it had been planted only three or four weeks earlier rather than like a two-month-old garden that should have been at its peak. Nature had told me in May that the growth would be held back until the end of the heavy rain cycle. What I didn't realize was that the rain cycle wasn't going to end until August! I found it increasingly difficult to keep my good humor about the ankle-deep water I was forever wading through.

In early August, I had what looked to be a complete "breakdown" with the squash family plants. They were infested with hundreds of squash bugs. Even though I was consulting with nature about the problem, I couldn't seem to get a handle on the situation. I realized the pressure was getting to me, so I sat down at the weekly meeting and asked nature for help. (The Calibration Process had not been developed at this time.) The following is that session.

NATURE SESSION

Garden Coning—3 August 1989
Re: Personal feelings plus working with Pan in new process

Machaelle: Well, I need help. I think the gardener is the key element that is out of balance. I'm trying so hard to move with you through this season's garden, yet I swing from confidence and exhilaration to terrific concern and despair. I see miracles all around me and then I see endless struggle that tends to end up in what looks to be failure. I feel pressure like I haven't felt in a long time. I'm trying to keep my focus on the garden as a research dynamic and not do things that will prove visually pleasing to people who come to see this garden. I'm finding this balance increasing difficult as the time for the Open House nears. I seem to be locked into wanting to demonstrate our partnership to others through the visual sense—mostly because I know that this is the sense that people rely on for confirmation when they come to Perelandra. I feel like so much is riding on what they see, or think they see. So I feel like I'm hanging on to this garden and not letting it have the freedom and flexibility it needs.

This is the macrocosm of how I'm feeling. The microcosm of it all is demonstrated in the squash bug situation. Somehow I feel I'm playing out all of my frustrations with the squash bugs—and I'm losing the battle, of course, and now I'm backed into a corner. It seems like nothing sets up a breakthrough better than being backed into a corner. I'm placing myself in your hands and asking what it is that I need to do in order to adjust myself and also to take the pressure off this garden so that it can balance and shine.

*Pan: I'd like to address what you have said. I speak for us all within the nature intelligences when I say that this garden is not under nearly the pressure you have perceived. **You** are indeed experiencing the sensations of pressure, but this has not been filtered into the garden patterns and rhythms.*

Let me address your personal feelings first. You have asked to move on with the nature research. You have, in fact, unlocked the door to the next level and you have moved to a level that is familiar because it still is nature, yet it is very new in its dynamics and movements. You have gone through several periods of personal and perceptual adjustments in order to be able to perceive the new. And you have moved along in this change and development at a rapid pace. Your dedication to moving on and facing all that this implies has been heartwarming to us and productive for you. It has also not been easy for you at times. Moving quickly through change and adjustment can leave one disoriented, physically uncomfortable, confused and sometimes in despair.

The "lid" you are feeling is not one that is sitting on top of the garden, thus not allowing the garden "to shine," as you so beautifully put it. The lid is within you.

You have already expressed fear that this new level which you have just entered will lead you into an area of understanding and research that will, in effect, detach you from the thrust of Perelandra as a viable teaching center for those who wish to work directly with nature. In short, you fear that the new level will spin you too far out, so to speak, and you will not be able to relate yourself or your work to those who look to you as a teacher. As I have said to you in our conversations lately, this is not true. You will always be able to relate both yourself and your knowledge to others simply by moving that which you have learned from your broader context to the less complex context of those who seek you out. As with the impact of the Workbook, what you will experience and learn will be transferable to others in other contexts.

Now, it is important that you not allow the context of others to limit you. This is the lid you are feeling and this is the cause of the pressure you are feeling. It is not the garden that is experiencing a lack of freedom and flexibility; it is you. And it is because you are trying mightily to function within a context that no longer serves you or Perelandra well. It is simply too confining. Your ring-pass-not expanded significantly once you unlocked the doors to this new level of research and work with nature. It will be important for you to allow the old context to slip away and the new to move into its place.

We suggest that you accomplish this by maintaining a focus on your work with us and disregard its implications regarding context. Simply by concentrating on working with us, moving with us, the old will disappear rapidly and the new will automatically form. People who come to Perelandra will continue to feel and see the results of working in partnership with nature. They will feel a very different atmosphere. They will not ask questions that will require you to explain your personal context, the personal level on which you are working, to them. They will not be able to perceive the specifics of what they are experiencing and will simply assume that whatever they are experiencing is a result of working with nature. That will be an excellent and workable conclusion, and it will serve to encourage them in their own partnership. This, after all, is the primary experience for which people come to the Perelandra garden.

It is important that you understand that you are not living in or functioning within the context of the reality that surrounds you outside Perelandra. It is important that you not allow that outside reality to dictate any element of the context in which you live and function. Your sense that it is important to address the visual needs of those who come to the Perelandra garden, so that they will receive the confirmation that they seek, is really one way you are allowing this outside reality to dictate to you and Perelandra. Your desire to assist people with confirmation so that they will be more inclined to work with nature on their own is from the heart, and we recognize this. But now, we suggest that you let go of this limitation. It's holding you down. If you release yourself to the new level of functioning, there will be plenty that will serve as confirmation for others—and it will have a power beyond anything you and others could imagine.

How you function and the level of work you are doing is really well beyond the prevailing context that enfolds Earth. You are a nature scientist who is working with new levels of cooperation with nature that extend beyond any one level. The fact that you are doing this research while on the planet called Earth is incidental. It simply is not relevant to anything other than to prove that one can truly do complex and expanded work that benefits many levels from a specific level that, in its prevailing understanding of reality, does not extend beyond a basic and simplistic context. As you move along in your work, it will become more vital that the Earth reality around you be ignored.

All along, you have assumed that your work would automatically fit into and enhance what is happening on Earth. And this has proven to be true. You have maintained your focus on the garden, you have not dispersed yourself or your work by responding to the prevailing expectations of what someone in your position should be doing and how, and your work has taken off in its impact anyway. Now with this new stage, don't let expectations centered around how you have functioned up to now lock you in. Keep your focus on the garden and the overall work—the rest will take care of itself.

Use visits by others to the Perelandra garden as an opportunity to observe how this garden can reach them and function as their confirmation. It will not be, nor has it ever been, just visual. They may enter the garden with an expectation of visual confirmation. That is what you have picked up on. But once they enter the garden environment, this expectation is immediately replaced with an overall experience that often takes them time to process and identify. Their limited expectation (visual) has been superseded by something much larger that catches them by surprise. This is why you often don't hear them comment about the garden. They simply don't know what to do with what is happening to them. So they remain quiet. Rather than spend time and energy hoping to satisfy their visual expectations, redirect your focus to observing their reactions and seeing how many ways this garden makes contact with others.

Machaelle: Do you sense that I have allowed the information you've given me to lift the lid under which I've been operating?

Pan: Yes. The pressure has released from your head, hasn't it?

Machaelle: Yes. Should I allow the insights to digest overnight and open another session tomorrow to get some specifics about the squash bug situation, or can we go on?

Pan: The garden work is primarily right on target. Your personal changes in the area of this new level are so quick that we have lately had to give you information in between the weekly sessions. You've moved well with this. Let me give you the information on what is needed now.

Do another atmospheric balancing. Once this is complete, remain in the coning but specifically link with me. Then move to the zucchini plants again and we will go through the process we attempted last week. The "lid" or confinements you have been functioning under lately allowed that work to be only partially successful. We'll do it again, and I'm sure you will feel the work clearly and see a difference in the results. We will work on all three plants. Once completed with the zucchini, move to the yellow squash hills and we will do the same work there.

Also, plant the green beans tonight or tomorrow, plus more beet seeds, kale and carrots. Giving us these tools will enable us to do the work needed to, as you say, put the shine on the garden. Leave the trenches open for awhile. If you like, you can cover them with a layer of sticks and some straw for esthetics. But allowing others to see the extreme weather conditions with which you have worked this year will be beneficial also. We leave this decision up to you.

One other thing: You can remove the pieces of wood from the zucchini area. We felt you had to see that this type of "organic gardening method" is no longer effective in the Perelandra garden. In essence, we are working together on a level well beyond organic gardening, and the many tricks and tips that have been used with success within that context no longer work within the Perelandra context. An organic gardener would not believe it if you told him that you put boards underneath the zucchini, and the bugs ignored them totally!

Doing the above things will move the garden right along a direct line with its present pattern and rhythm and will also reflect in the garden the personal changes you've made as a result of today's insights. Everything will be current and synchronized. Unless you have any remaining questions, we will close for now and let you get ready for your game of racquetball.

Machaelle: I can't think of any questions. I sense that I'll want to have sessions more frequently just to keep myself and the garden moving in concert.

Pan: That will be fine. Being consciously connected with us while working in the garden will be essential also. I would especially like to continue our new work together.

Machaelle: Me, too. With that, I will close the coning. Thank you.

Pan: You are most welcome. (Close coning.)

Right after this session, the rains stopped and the garden "took off." By the Open House, it was flourishing and at the peak of its maturity. I had lettuce that I had planted in May (these were the seeds that had been under 3 inches of water) that was now maturing and most edible. It was a garden that completely defied reason—even my sense of reason.

The squash-bug situation ended up being part of the initial experiments nature had set up which eventually, in 1990, led to the development of the Insect Triangulation Process and the Troubleshooting Process.

A PERSONAL NOTE: I have included this more personal session with nature because I feel that the concerns, fears and thoughts I expressed in the session are common to all of us co-creative gardeners from time to time. For example, when others hear about the unusual successes we are having, they want to come look at the garden. You may not have hundreds of people showing up for an open house like we do, but I feel certain that when a handful of folks ask to see your garden—each arriving with his or her own set of expectations—you'll understand what I'm talking about in the session. I hope this window into my struggles will help you as you move through similar experiences.

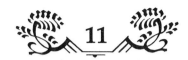

Troubleshooting

You have gotten word from the garden meeting that something needs troubleshooting, or everything in the garden is humming along fine and suddenly, without warning, a plant collapses or a row is being totally devoured by insects. You scratch your head and say something profound like "Huh?" This calls for quick action, but you haven't the vaguest idea where to start.

Before, when I was faced with, shall we say, a "sudden turn," I would mentally go through a list with nature of all the processes and approaches I could remember to see what I should do. To be frank, it was a hit-and-miss proposition that was often fueled by my sense of panic. I felt like I was floundering all over the place. Nature and I needed a way to troubleshoot a problem in an organized way. This is what nature came up with, and I have to tell you, it's brilliant, not to mention simple.

GARDEN SESSION
Garden Coning—27 July 1990

We are ready now to work with you in an organized troubleshooting (as you call it) procedure. We suggest the steps of the process be as follows:

1. Open a 4-pt. coning including the overlighting deva of the specialized environment in which the problem is occurring. Include also the deva of the plant, animal, mineral or other form that has the problem. Balance and stabilize the coning. One does not need to be physically present at the site of the problem in order to do the troubleshooting. One need only be personally focused on the issue. Testing for personal flower essence needs after the coning is balanced and stabilized and before commencing with the troubleshooting process would assure that the individual is clear.

2. State the intent to troubleshoot a problem situation with the specific form that is involved.

3. The very first question to ask is whether the form in trouble needs to be replaced with another form. As there is natural miscarriage within the animal kingdom when form, for one reason or another, has been damaged or diseased to such an extent that appropriate life rhythms would be impossible, there is also natural "miscarriage" within the other nature kingdoms. In gardening and farming, the troubleshooting would most likely occur with the plant kingdom. For other types of form, it is still appropriate to ask if the form needs to be replaced. With inanimate objects, the need to replace the form would imply that the form does not correspond with the intent or its purpose. Although this is true with any form replacement, it may be difficult for people to understand that the form and intent/purpose balance also applies to inanimate objects.

If the answer is yes, then we suggest that questions about change in type of form (different variety of plant, etc.), replacement preparation and timing be asked. It is not wise to assume that replacement will be immediate, especially with perennial plants. Soil preparation may be necessary. In short, if replacement is suggested, the person will need to approach this issue as if planting for the first time and move through the various placement and preparation processes in the Workbook.

If the answer is no, this means that the present form is acceptable and the troubleshooting process should be continued.

4. An individual does not need to identify the problem in order to troubleshoot it. We will know the problem, and, most likely, our interpretation of the difficulty will be different from what humans have perceived the problem to be from their studies and observation. In a co-creative environment, a problem is looked at from many more different levels and angles than in a traditional, 5-senses-dominant environment.

However, if one wishes, for his own understanding, to know what a specific problem is, he need only read through a listing of the insect problems and diseases about the plants in question. (We are now focusing on plants since this is the issue we are addressing today. The intent of what we are talking about extends to any form of troubleshooting.)

We recommend that if a problem is identified, the suggested listing of remedies not be assumed as the course of action we in nature will propose be taken. Some of the suggested remedies might very well be a part of the course of action, but, most likely, a number of other suggestions will be brought forward that are not known in traditional agricultural circles.

5. Whether the problem is known by the individual or not, begin identifying the course of action by testing a basic list of possible environmental needs such as:

    Watering
    Too much sun/too little sun
    Wind damage: need for protection
    Soil fertilizing
    Foliar feeding
    Interplanting needed or changed
    Pruning

Before *supplying these environmental needs, continue the troubleshooting by testing a list of energy-level needs:*

    Energy Cleansing Process
    Battle Energy Release
    Soil Balancing & Stabilizing:
        The specialized environment generally
        The problem plant and its immediate soil
    Atmospheric balancing
    Geopathic Zone balancing
    Flower essences foliar feeding:
        A solution for a plant or system generally
        A solution for the problem specifically
    Plant triangulation balancing and stabilizing
    Insect balancing and stabilizing
        Check this whether insects are prevalent or not.
    Insect triangulation check

Calibration Process:
> *For the gardener*
> *For the plant or other form involved*

6. Once the course of action has been identified, it will be important to ascertain the order the steps are to be done in. More often than not, the steps will all be done within the same time period. Sometimes, one or a couple of the steps will precede the others and a waiting period will be needed in between. All of this information can be gotten through kinesiology testing.

7. Proceed through the steps as indicated. If there is a waiting period between steps, it will be important to ascertain whether the plant, for example, will need to be covered or protected during this period.

Once the steps are completed:
> *Test for protection needs and for how long.*
> *Test for follow-up troubleshooting.*
>> *How soon should it be done?*
> *Test for stabilizing essences to be used during a "convalescence" period.*
>> *Used for how long?*

8. Allow the plant involved to proceed through its healing and balancing process. If questions come up as to whether the plant is in additional trouble or unforeseen difficulty, an individual can open the coning (as it is opened for the troubleshooting session) and ask if anything further needs to be done. We perceive that the major difficulty during this waiting period will be around an individual's interference. No matter how good the intentions, it will still be interference.

9. Do all the follow-up testing and work as scheduled. For perennial plants, we see that there will most likely be a period of time beyond anything being done specifically for the plant, after the plant is looking well again, in which a flower essence stabilizing solution will be applied. This will be important for stabilizing the plant back into its balanced rhythms and patterns.

1. Open a 4-pt. coning + overlighting deva of the environment in which the problem occurs + deva of specific plant/animal/form that has the problem.
Balance and stabilize the coning, and check yourself for essences.

2. State your intent to troubleshoot a problem.

3. Ask if the present form should be replaced. If yes:
Change in form/variety?
Replacement preparation and timing information.

4. Identify or attempt to identify the problem using information from a good gardening/plant encyclopedia, or other source appropriate to the problem.

5. **Environmental Troubleshooting List:**
Watering
Too much sun/too little sun
Wind damage: need for protection
Soil fertilizing needed: What and how much?
Foliar feeding needed: What and how much?
Interplanting needed or changed
Pruning needed
Other
Energy-Level Troubleshooting List:
Energy Cleansing Process
Battle Energy Release Process
Soil Balancing and Stabilizing:
Specialized environment generally
Problem plant and its immediate soil
Atmospheric Balancing Process
Geopathic Zone Process
Flower Essences Foliar Feeding:
Solution for a plant or form system generally
Solution for the specific problem
Plant Triangulation
Insect Balancing and Stabilizing

Check this whether insects are prevalent or not.
Insect Triangulation
Calibration Process: For the gardener? For the form involved?

6. Order of needed steps.
Waiting period between?
Should plant/form be covered/protected during waiting period?
Complete steps as set up.

7. Test for protection needs and for how long.
Test for follow-up troubleshooting.
　　When?
Test for stabilizing essences solution and dosage.

8. This process is now complete. Thank your team, close the coning and test yourself for essences and dosage.

9. Allow plant to proceed through healing and balancing process.

10. Do all follow-up testing and work as scheduled. Check for flower essences stabilizing solution at the end of the troubleshooting period.

NOTE: On the next page, you will see that I have put together a chart for doing this process. As with the blank charts in the *Workbook*, I suggest that you xerox copies of this one before using it.

When I first got this process from nature, I had to smile. All of a sudden, I saw the last 2-1/2 years' work coming together. It was as if nature had "aimed" for the Troubleshooting Process all along. With this process, nature ties all of the other processes together and creates a cohesive and comprehensive approach that is designed to meet each specific need or problem.

To me, the focus of this process's brilliance is step 6—ordering the steps. That's where nature designs a specific treatment program. And this is where I "sit back and watch" experts at work. I have found the programs they design to be awesome in both approach and results. And I feel that, with the Troubleshooting Process, we move to a new level in our co-creative partnership with nature.

HINT: Don't limit doing the Troubleshooting Process to just the growing season. If you have problem areas or a tree, bush or other perennial in trouble, test to see if you need to Troubleshoot them in winter. Nature will begin a treatment program with one or more of the energy processes. This will prepare the way for continuing the treatment in spring with the environmental processes and/or more energy processes.

Co-Creative Troubleshooting Process Chart

Plant: _____ Date: _____

1. 4-point coning + _____

2. State intent to troubleshoot problem.

3. Replace form: _____ yes _____ no
   Change variety/form: _____
   Replacement preparation/timing: _____

4. Identify/describe problem: _____

5. *Environmental Troubleshooting List:*

___ Watering: _____
___ Too much sun/too little sun: _____
___ Wind damage: need for protection/relocation: _____
___ Soil fertilizing needed (what and how much): _____
   _____
___ Foliar feeding needed (dosage): _____
___ Interplanting needed or changed: _____
___ Pruning/surgery: _____
___ Additional needs: _____
___ _____
___ _____

Energy Process Troubleshooting List:

___ Energy Cleansing Process:
   Bal/Stab: _____
___ Battle Energy Release Process:
   Bal/Stab: _____
   Soil Balancing and Stabilizing:
___   Specific environment (general):
      Bal/Stab: _____
___   Problem plant and its immediate soil:
      Bal/Stab: _____
___ Atmospheric Balancing:
      Bal/Stab: _____
   Flower Essences Foliar Feeding:
___   General solution for plant's system:
      Sol/Dosage: _____
___   Solution for specific problem. Telegraph test.
      Problem 1 Sol/Dosage: _____
      Problem 2 Sol/Dosage: _____
      Problem 3 Sol/Dosage: _____
      Problem 4 Sol/Dosage: _____
___ Plant Triangulation: Triangle Points: _____
   Bal/Stab: _____
___ Insect Balancing (Check this whether insects are prevalent or not.)
   Bal/Stab: _____
___ Insect Triangulation: Triangle Points: _____
   Bal/Stab: _____
___ Calibration Process: _____ Gardener _____ Plant _____ Soil _____ Insect _____ Other
   Essences or Bal/Stab: _____
___ Geopathic Zone Balancing:
   Energy Cleansing Bal/Stab: _____
   Battle Energy Release Bal/Stab: _____
   Soil Balancing Bal/Stab: _____

6. Order the steps. (Place order of steps to left of list.)

7. Waiting period between steps: _____ no _____ yes
    How long: _____

8. Protection needed during waiting period: _____ no _____ yes
    What: _____

9. Post-work protection: _____ no _____ yes
    What: _____
    How long: _____

10. Troubleshooting stabilizing essences & dosage: _____

11. Follow-up troubleshooting date: _____

Record follow-up data below.

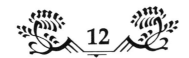

Final Thoughts

Sometimes people think that working with nature provides unquestioned, undeniable "perfection." (We're back to the forty-pound smiling cabbages and singing rabbits here.) "After all," they reason, "nature is this all-knowing, powerful intelligence capable of accomplishing anything. So working with them will be a snap and, in perhaps a half-hour's time, nature will make my garden perfect. Besides, my heart's in the right place."

I keep using the word "perfect." I'd like to point out some things about "perfect." First of all, perfect is not a single point, level or state that we all have agreed on. Perfect is relative to whoever is defining or decreeing. It is solely based on that individual's notion, and I find that, oftentimes, it is intimately linked with what they think heaven will be. It frequently includes doing no work and having finger-tip abundance. In a garden, perfect also frequently means there are no insects to bother either us or our food. And, of course, nature is there to do our bidding.

As ludicrous as all this may sound, it is an attitude that I find fairly common among people who are attracted to the concept of working with nature. It's something I'd like to address head on because those who hold it are way off the mark.

To those gardeners who wish to work with nature and still hold onto the notion of instant perfection, let me point out that the co-creative garden is worked with nature *in partnership*. I know I have pointed this out often, but it is a concept that needs to be clarified in order to begin to understand what is required on our part. In a partnership, we have two separate and distinct individuals—the gardener and nature—each with his own areas of responsibility and expertise. Together they create a team. One does not do all the work while the other kicks back in a hammock and thinks up ideas. Both work and both think—and both seek agreement with each other.

The purpose of the partnership is to work with nature for the betterment of all concerned. This calls for a lot of healing and building. Consequently, when we work with nature through the environmental and energy processes, the results focus around healing, balancing, strengthening and building—not some heaven-like perfection. The former has to do with reality and life dynamics; the latter is myth.

One of the things I have noticed about working co-creatively with nature in the garden is that everything is in a state of constant change, constant flux. I can see, after watching this for so many years, that the changes are all centered around healing, balancing, strengthening and building. However, often, when I was in the midst of a change, I didn't see all this. It was only after seeing how seemingly unrelated actions, a process here and another process there, all hook together and result in mind-boggling improvement that I was able to see it. We may be doing seemingly unrelated little things over a period of two or three years that won't make a lick of sense to us until the third or fourth year when it all comes together.

Those of us who have practiced co-creative gardening tend to know what I am talking about. We understand that the co-creative garden is in constant process. It's never static. And there are times when we are doing everything we are supposed to do and *know* that the garden is right on target—but it *looks* awful. Nature suggested that this year there should have been no tilling between rows, and you are now looking at a crop of weeds standing about four-feet high. You haven't the vaguest idea what is going on—I often don't know what's going on—and someone from your office who has heard that you do an "interesting" kind of gardening with "them deevas and elves" has dropped by for a visit. They look at this "mess" and, although they may be polite, you can tell they are disgusted.

This is something all co-creative gardeners have to contend with. We co-creative folks know that whatever is happening at a particular moment is somehow healing, balancing, strengthening and building the garden environment in ways we may not understand. We only know in our gut that it's happening. We can feel it and we can see a change in the garden activity that verifies it. That visitor hasn't the vaguest notion of what is going on. Nine times out of ten, they are looking at your garden through their lens of perfection—and they expect to see the National Botanical Garden. Understand what they are doing and don't let that outside reaction influence your partnership with nature.

In case you are thinking that co-creative gardening is synonymous with mess, let me assure you that it isn't. I am often struck between the eyes at the beauty and balance of the Perelandra garden. And I am amazed at the beauty nature has programmed into the garden in ways I never would have thought of. If I had to characterize the co-creative garden, I would say that it is an extraordinary balance between beauty and change—constant beauty and constant change. And then I would add that all of life's dynamics are portrayed to the highest degree and intensity.

I have presented these energy processes within the context of gardening and agriculture. The laboratory in which the processes are worked out at Perelandra happens to be a garden. But let me give you some points to ponder.

Nature energy is everywhere. Everything that is form is nature. You may not live in the country or work a garden. You may not even have a potted plant. You may be surrounded by concrete and glass, and you may be inundated with the constant rumble of traffic noise. The concrete and glass are products derived from nature. A car's components all come from combinations of elements listed on the Periodic Chart of the Elements. Remember that chart? That was the chart you had to look at throughout tenth-grade chemistry. You swore you would never think about that chart again. Well, it's back to haunt you.

Everything that is in form is composed of either elements straight from that chart or compounds of those elements. Usually when I say this to people, their eyes glass over and I hear a collective internal scream coming from them: "Oh yeah, lady. Whadda 'bout plastics?!" Well, I looked up plastics. They are nothing more than combinations of hydrogen, carbon and oxygen molecules that have been strung together by a process called "polymerization" that creates compounds of high molecular weight called "polymers." We humans figured out how to combine hydrogen, oxygen and carbon atoms—all natural elements straight from that chart—to create something that is not found in the wild. We humans have this tendency. Don't forget that we did essentially the same thing to create a garden. We combined natural elements—soil, plants, seeds, water, air, fertilizers—to create something that isn't found in the wild.

Of course there is a debate here. Just because natural elements can be combined, should they? This isn't the issue I'm attempting to address now. I will say this, however. Imagine what might have happened in that chemistry lab when the concept of polymerization was discovered had the chemist been working with nature in partnership. I'll bet you that the plastic compound would have been biodegradable from the beginning, because nature would not have recommended a combination of elements that would have created form that was so far removed from the overall natural planetary rhythms.

So, everything that is in form is comprised of natural elements. And where there is nature, there is an opportunity for a partnership between us and nature.

But nature is more than the Periodic Chart of the Elements. That just gives us the form that interacts with our five senses. According to nature's definitions, form exists where there is order, organization and life vitality. And nature is responsible for and creates all of form's order, organization and life vitality. Consequently, where there is order, organization and life vitality, there is nature. A creative thought is an electrical impulse that has been initiated by us and then ordered, organized and given life vitality; therefore, it is now in a *form* we call "thought."

We are back to the involution/evolution balance I mentioned in chapter 1. We humans supply the spirit, intent, direction, free-will decisions and the soul-infused needs. Nature supplies the dynamics for the medium and the method (technique and process) for translating all of these soul-originated impulses into useful form. The balance between involution and evolution occurs when the involution acts as a perfectly fitted glove to the soul hand. When this occurs, there is no sense of limitation. There is only pure spirit reflected fully through completely appropriate form. We are here on Earth, in form, to learn what is required for us to strike this balance between involution and evolution dynamics. There is an implied partnership with nature in this challenge.

We humans have only half of the picture and half of the input. Nature is the expert on the other half of the picture. We can either allow the partnership to function while we remain unconscious to its development, or we can "turn to nature" and consciously ask, "What do I need and how should I proceed in order to establish an involution/evolution balance in the various areas of my life?"

In short, we make a silent partner into a conscious partner. With both partnerships, there is a movement towards involution/evolution balance. This, after all, is the natural order of things. But the unconscious partnership is similar in dynamic to any partnership where we choose not to acknowledge the importance, input, existence or expertise of the other partner. As a partnership, it limps along despite itself. In a conscious partnership, you've got communication, coordination and flexibility going on. It's an exciting dynamic—and it's efficient.

So now we have a potential partnership with nature that is inherent in all form. And we have a potential partnership in our personal efforts to strike an involution/evolution balance in our lives. But there's another partnership I'd like to point out, and this one leads me directly back to the energy processes in this book.

Energy is form. Remember, nature said that energy is just form that we can't perceive with our five senses. All form operates within the same overall universal principles. (That's why the processes I develop in the garden arena can be equally applied to other arenas outside of the garden. A process that works within the garden-form context will also work within another form context—like a classroom, or a home, or an apartment building or a dental lab . . .) Negative, inappropriate or out-of-balance energy has as much of an ecological impact as sulfur emissions, toxic waste and nuclear fallout. It's just that with energy pollution we can't see it, so we tend not to address it. In actuality, most folks don't even know it's there or that their environment is deteriorating just as rapidly from energy pollution as from five-senses pollution. We, personally, are impacted by energy pollution in fundamental ways.

When energy impacts an environment, it alters that environment's form. It either enhances and supports that environment or it weakens and deteriorates it. But an energy cannot be introduced into any form reality without altering that larger reality. It becomes part of the larger mix, and the larger reality shifts to accommodate that energy. Consequently, an environment becomes a self-sustaining biosphere that is made up of a combination of all of the related elements contained within it. Perelandra is an environmental biosphere. Your suburban property or your apartment building and its land are other biospheres. The energy processes in this book address biosphere balancing and management.

Generally, when I talk to others about these concepts, they can grasp the importance of environmental balance. After all, we are finally in the age of ecology. But what they don't grasp right away is the impact these environments or biospheres have on the ability of the people within them to function. If it's out of sight and out of mind, like the ozone layer, what possible impact could it have on our everyday lives? So let me give you a couple of examples that I've run across.

I knew a fellow who was going through a particularly strange and vitriolic divorce. He was completely caught off guard when his wife suddenly ended the marriage and moved out in a somewhat dramatic manner. What was strange was that she kept returning when he wasn't around to dig up plants and perennials in all of the gardens and beds. He said that whenever he returned, the property felt like something had been ripped out of it. He also said that he felt that she was acting out her anger on the land. When he heard about the work I was doing at Perelandra, he asked me if there was something I could do that would be helpful to the land.

I worked from a well-drawn map of their property which placed the woods, swamp, fields, house, driveway and gardens. It was an isolated piece of land—about thirty-five acres—that was way in the country. I set up a coning and did the Energy Cleansing Process, Battle Energy Release and Soil Balancing and Stabilizing. From the flower essence stabilizers that were needed, it was clear to me that part of the battle energy that was released was the divorce. In fact, there was so much energy-process activity around the house and garden areas that I suggested to him that he do a little research and find out the history of the house regarding previous owners.

He got back to me several weeks later. It seems that the house had remained empty for a number of years prior to their purchasing and restoring it. But he was able to find out that the family who had owned the house before them had gone through a divorce that had exactly the same dynamics: the wife left suddenly and unexpectedly, the process was especially vitriolic and she kept returning to rip up the gardens.

We don't know what the history was prior to this couple. But I can say that the energy that was released by them around this divorce didn't just dissipate into nothingness. It had to go somewhere. From my previous work with nature and the Battle Energy Release Process, I knew that nature absorbs ungrounded, unprocessed, emotional energy which, in turn, buffers us from being constantly battered by a planetary environment of everyone's emotional releases. What also happens is that the form that absorbs such energy shifts *accommodates* the existence of that energy in its overall reality. In short, the molecular makeup of the form has altered to accommodate the new energy. There is a universal principle that nature repeats to me over and over: like attracts like. When you have an environment that has contained within it the energy elements of particular human action and interaction, that environment then supports that kind of action.

I'm not saying that the history of the land caused these two people to divorce. Most likely, they would have divorced anyway. But what the land did do was enhance and support those feelings and actions that had already been played out at least once in this house. Without realizing it, these two people automatically adjusted their thinking and actions in a manner that was supported by the energy makeup of their biosphere. Their personal options in moving through the separation and divorce became limited.

The energy-process work that I did appropriately released the various energy elements that were part of their biosphere that did not enhance balance. And then, through the use of the balancing and stabilizing processes, nature and I moved that biosphere into a life-enhancing balance. (By the way, once I completed this work, the wife no longer returned to dig up the gardens.) It now would not draw to it two people who had the potential of repeating the same things that had already been acted out by the previous two owners. A future couple may divorce, but it will be processed differently.

Another example: I have a friend who runs a firm that trains and assists inner-city project residents to take over the management and eventual ownership of their own buildings. These projects are usually one step away from total collapse in every way. The residents must be taught a variety of management skills from financial considerations down to the smallest of maintenance skills. On the whole, my friend's firm has success and is recognized in the community as being a successful alternative to inner-city housing problems. But the success is often hard fought.

Well, as I listened to my friend describe the problems, I could tell that the residents they were working with were perfectly capable of learning the necessary skills and taking over the project management. They were not stupid people. But her firm was meeting with all kinds of resistance from these people. In some cases, it was like trying to pull their feet out of tar. All of the projects are in areas of the city that are run down and low income. There is a high crime rate and a lot of drug dealing. These kinds of problems have existed in these areas for many years.

I kept saying to her that she had a problem with how the people and the building and its land were interacting. On the one hand, her firm was attempting to assist the people to make a major step forward in how they lived their lives. On the other hand, the buildings they lived in and the land upon which the buildings sat were physically supporting the very things the people were trying to move away from. It's as if a totally sane person was locked up in our worst nightmare of a mental institution and was not only expected to continue to act sanely but also to make significant progress in a new discipline. It's not fair to ask or expect someone to function in exceptional ways under these conditions. My friend had to change the balance of the environment so that it enhanced and supported the new.

Another point: These residents had already committed themselves to changing and taking charge of their situation. It was clear from their actions that, as they opened up to the intent of their commitment, they became more sensitive. And, their ability to move forward became more hampered. The personal issues they needed to face in order to affect these changes were magnified by the various comparable emotional energies that were already present in their environment. Their personal difficulties became magnets to these energies—like attracting like. Again, it was doubly difficult for the residents to personally change because what they were attempting to move away from was constantly being energized by their environment.

To be honest, my friend thought I was nuts—mildly nuts—when I told her what I thought needed to be done. At best, I was obsessing and trying to push this nature business off on her. But because she was my friend, I took the liberty to keep chipping away at her. Eventually, I said the right words and she heard them. Conceptually, she then understood that these people were being held back because of all the energy patterns that were part of their environment. She bought a Soil Balancing Kit, read about the three energy processes in the *Workbook* (*Workbook II* had not yet been written) and went back to the city to try working with nature.

I got a call from her a couple of weeks later. She did the three energy processes at her office first. Immediately, people began relating to one another differently. She needed to make some difficult personnel changes anyway, and the process resulted in a smaller, tighter, more efficient team. She also needed to reorganize her office, and that process also worked in ways that defied reason.

She already knew kinesiology and had been working with flower essences for years. So she had the tools in place for making contact and working with nature in this new partnership. She used the simple yes/no format with nature. She was instructed to set up conings, make small models of all of the projects her firm had contracts for and to collect small soil samples from the grounds of each project. She was then to place the soil samples in the models. From her office, she was to set up the coning and work with nature to soil balance and stabilize each of the projects.

She worked with one huge project first. It had a total of fifteen buildings. She had a soil sample from each of the buildings' grounds, plus she was told to put a sample from the fifteen grounds into the centrally located common-ground area in the model. She worked with nature to first energy cleanse the whole site, do the Battle Energy Release for the entire site and then balance and stabilize each building and its land. Whatever was needed, she just dropped a small amount onto the soil sample in the model.

Various things happened within days of her work. For one thing, she had to meet with the local electric company to ask for an extension regarding funding so that energy conservation training could be extended throughout the entire project. This was important because as the people moved into the newly renovated apartments, they had to assume the energy bills. Up till then, these bills had always been included in the rent. Without the training, the tenants would experience severe money traumas from the high energy bills. My friend was anticipating a real problem with the electric company—in fact, she was expecting a confrontation. Instead, they informed her, as she walked in the door, that they were giving both her and this project an extension. Kiss that confrontation goodbye. Not only this, but her firm also got, at the same time, the final approval for the increased training funds from the government *after* the government had already rejected the funding in writing. They had, on their own, reversed themselves and decided that the funding would come out of capital expenses and that it was considered an investment in the future.

Then five days after the energy work, there was an open house at the project. She said it was great. For the first time, the residents helped support the existing management in the new direction, and the owners acknowledged and supported this new direction, recognizing the residents as future owners.

Since this time, progress in that particular project has moved by leaps and bounds. The residents, along with the owners and management, came up with the idea of using the common ground to establish the first inner-city plant and tree nursery and to work together to make it a money-making venture. The existing owner has already contracted a landscape architect/nursery fellow to joint-venture with the residents and help set up the program. In short, this particular housing project is well on its way to becoming a model program.

My friend is now working with nature on the other projects her firm is responsible for. She has seen such dramatic results that I don't think anything would stop her from incorporating this partnership with nature into her work. She's operating in the "straight world" and isn't talking about what she is doing, of course. She's not stupid. She's letting the results speak for themselves and she is only answering the questions that people are asking. She's also working on a way that this nature information and work can be taught to the residents without infringing on their personal belief systems. Ideally, it would be best if the residents took over the responsibility of maintaining the energy balance of their own environment.

And from the department of "like attracting like:" My friend attended a conference in Switzerland this past year. While there, she got into a conversation with a fellow that led to sharing information about her nature work. He ended up asking her to help him and his group clear out, balance and stabilize a large building they had been given to convert into an international peace studies center. It had once been part of a Nazi concentration camp during World War II.

So, what am I suggesting here? First of all, you don't have to be a gardener or farmer to work with nature and the processes in both the *Workbook* and *Workbook II*. If you would like to function well and do something profoundly important for the health and well-being of your immediate environment, you will need to work co-creatively with the environmental and energy processes for the home and business environments where you live and operate.

AN IMPORTANT SIDE NOTE: We can only take responsibility for those environments where we are the custodians or where we have been asked by the custodian to do this work. In an apartment building, unless you have a contract such as my friend's firm had, you only have responsibility for your apartment. Do the processes just within that area. In an office, focus on your office space or, if you are the manager or owner, the entire office complex. If you are a teacher and wish to balance your class environment, you will focus only on your classroom, not on the entire school. You do not need a soil sample—there wouldn't be one in the middle of an office on the tenth floor. Just focus on the space you are responsible for as if it created an environment unto itself. (Working from a good floor plan or layout of the space will help you maintain focus and work with precision with nature.) This is your garden. To assume responsibility for someone else's environment would be manipulative both to that person and to the nature intelligences working with that person, albeit unconsciously, and his environment. I urge you to concentrate only on what is your responsibility or what has been specifically asked of you, and to resist any I'm-going-to-balance-the-world-all-by-myself impulses. Trust me: When you concentrate with nature on your own environment, it creates a ripple effect that automatically impacts the people around you. Suddenly, you'll see your neighbor do things you never believed he would have considered doing.

HINT: If you're having trouble finding privacy in a public environment to do these processes, you have one excellent place available that assures you privacy— the bathroom!

One last thought: The following is a reprint from the *Workbook*. I feel it is appropriate to include this session in *Workbook II* because

Workbook II is an extension of the *Workbook*, and what the Overlighting Deva of Planet Earth said applies equally to the intent and direction of *Workbook II*. I also feel that it is important to read this session with our new understanding of the words "nature," "form" and "garden" and what the nature intelligences mean when *they* use these words. The Overlighting Deva of Planet Earth never meant for nature to just mean a tree, form to mean only what we can see and touch, and a garden only to mean that little piece of land from which we harvest green beans.

OVERLIGHTING DEVA OF PLANET EARTH

I have looked forward to this moment, to the opportunity to add to the effort being made through the vehicle of this book. I am the overlighting consciousness of the planet upon which you live. I have been referred to as "Gaia" by many. I would like to give you insight into the physical evolution of the planet as seen from my perspective.

All that exists in the solar system of which planet Earth is a part and in the countless realms and dimensions beyond is presently moving through a major shift. This you refer to as the movement from the Piscean era to the Aquarian era. Earth is not an out-of-step planet struggling within an in-step universe to reach the level of perfection that surrounds it. It is quite a common thing for humans on Earth to perceive themselves as lesser, behind in development and out of step. This very notion is what one may call "Piscean" in its dynamic. It sets up the planet and those souls who are choosing to experience the lessons of form in a parent/child situation—the universe being the parent, the planet and its inhabitants being the child. It was an important dynamic of the Piscean era, this continuous sense of the child striving and moving forward toward the all-knowing parent, and a dynamic which was played out in one way or another on every level of interaction on Earth. The notion of the parent served as the impetus to keep the child moving forward in the hope that one day, after much work and growth, the child would attain the peer position with the parent.

The parent/child notion has not been exclusive to Earth. It is a dynamic that has been part of reality on all other dimensions and levels. And as already stated, it has been an important dynamic of the Piscean era for the souls on all levels to come to grips with in whatever manner needed. I point this out to emphasize that Earth is part of an ever-evolving whole and not the bastard child of that whole.

The important lesson to be integrated into the picture of reality from the parent/child dynamic was the conscious, personal dedication of the individual to move forward. The parent dynamic stood before the child within all and encouraged those vital steps forward toward the perceived notion of perfection represented by the parent. It served to weave into the individual's fabric of life that sense of constant forward motion and the knowing that its resulting change led to something better and greater.

Although the parent/child dynamic has been a tangible force that has permeated the levels of reality during the Piscean era, the actual fact of every individual being the child seeking to move toward a parent has been illusion. It is how a Piscean dynamic was translated into a workable reality. An impulse was released within all levels of reality some two thousand years ago, and each individual receiving the impulse translated it into an understandable, tangible concept. The main thrust of the overall translation on planet Earth has been the parent/child dynamic. There has been, in fact, no parent outside and beyond who has enticed and encouraged the children forward. Just as the child is within all, so, too, is the parent. But in order to develop the tools they needed to move forward in confidence, individuals needed to establish that sense of the all-knowing parent standing before them in the unknown, ready to catch, comfort and receive them as they take those shaky steps forward.

I have not forgotten to address the planet Earth. I needed to lay the foundation for you to understand how the principles presented in this book fit into the larger picture—and that includes Earth.

When the impulse of what I have referred to as "the parent/child dynamic" was released throughout reality, it was received not only by individual human souls, but by the planet as a whole. I have stated that the impulse was sounded on all levels of reality. In order for there to be harmonious evolution, there must be a sense of tandem movement within the whole. The impulse was received and seated within planet Earth, which, in turn, stabilized the seating of the impulse within individuals. Now, as human souls translated that impulse into the workable parent/child dynamic, that translation itself seated into the planet and its various natural forms, thus modifying the original impulse to conform to the translation. This is natural law—form conforming to the energy within. It is a necessary part of the support system between spirit and matter. One cannot have the spirit reflecting one reality seated within a form energized by another reality. It would be as if two horses were hitched to one another but pulling in opposite directions. There would be no chance of forward movement. So, form must conform in order for there to be mutual support and evolution between matter and spirit.

To broaden this picture even more, let me say that the impulse and the translation of the impulse (as with all the Piscean impulses and their translations) placed the individuals and the planet squarely and solidly into the evolutionary picture of its universe as a whole—not out of step with it. The planet has been an active participant in understanding and working with what we might call "contemporary issues," for the issues have been the same throughout reality; only the translations have differed. It has been vital that the specific parent/child translation, for example, be fully explored and understood by those on Earth so that the resulting knowledge could be made accessible to the whole. Likewise, other translations of the very same impulse have been made accessible to the whole and have been received at various times throughout the Piscean era by individuals and the intelligences of nature on Earth.

Now a new set of impulses has been sounded throughout reality, and they are the impulses commonly referred to as "Aquarian." All of reality has moved into a period of transition. The impulses are in the process of being fully seated in and translated everywhere. On Earth, we have full reception of the initial Aquarian impulses. They are seated well within the planet and are now serving the shift of those living on the planet from Piscean to Aquarian.

If you have followed my train of thought, you will realize that with the planet itself holding the Aquarian impulses, all that exists on the planet and all its individuals are not only receiving the similar impulses but the impetus and support from the planet to change, as well. This means that those translations and the resulting systems and procedures from the old simply will not function as smoothly in the present. The soul energy of the planet has shifted and no longer correlates with the old form translations that exist on its surface. And very shortly, you will see a rapid deterioration of all that has worked so well in the past. New translations are required. New systems and procedures. The planet is already holding the new impulses.

The co-creative gardening processes as presented in this book are a translation of the new. They work because they once again align spirit and matter with parallel intent and purpose. In this case, one could say we have a double alignment. We have the spirit of the human translating impulse into new form and action, and we have the connection of the spirit of the human with the new impulses contained within the planet around him. As you incorporate these translations into thought and action, you will see evidence of effortless change all around you. As already stated, this is because the intent of spirit and the intent of matter are realigning and once again moving in tandem.

This brings me back to the parent/child notion of the Piscean era. One of the translations of this dynamic from humans has been in the arena of nature. That is, humans have tended to look at nature either as the parent looking at a child in need of discipline, or the child seeking beneficial aid and assistance from the powerful and all-knowing parent. In essence, humans have translated the parent/child dynamic in nature as either manipulation or worship. Both translations were working, viable frameworks for learning, but they are both no longer workable. For humans to continue attempting to respond and to act within these two mindsets is wreaking havoc on the planet itself.

With the Aquarian dynamic, the parent/child is uniting as one balanced, integrated force within the individual. It is the uniting of the universal wisdom contained within all and the absolute knowledge that in order to have full, conscious access to that universal wisdom, one must continue to move forward in the learning and changing mode. The parent and child come together in balanced partnership.

The co-creative garden translates this fundamental Aquarian dynamic into the arena of nature. Human and nature come together in conscious, equal partnership, both functioning from a position of wisdom and change. Wherever such a garden is initiated, it will immediately sound a note outward into the universe and inward into the core of the planet, the very soul of the planet, that the shift from Piscean to Aquarian dynamics within that nature arena is in the process of change. And immediately, the evolving intent of the garden will be aligned with the prevailing universal flow and the corresponding planetary impulses, one buttressing from above, the other buttressing from below within the planet. The result will be forward motion in tandem—the gardener in tandem with his planet and his universe. With this massive support, it is no wonder the co-creative garden works.

Allow me to give you another insight. The Aquarian impulses are already seated within the planet. Visualize, if you will, the planet as a container of these impulses—energy held beneath the Earth's surface. This energy is seated within the very soul of the planet, seated within its heart. It is there to be released and integrated into all levels of life on the planet. Now, picture one, small co-creative garden on the planet's surface. See it as a window into the interior of the planet, into its soul. As the gardener works to align this garden to the new dynamics, watch the window open and the energy contained within the core of the planet gently gravitate to and release through the window. Feel the sense of relief and freedom within the Earth's core as the energy moves upward and out. And watch the actions and the form on the Earth's surface suddenly shift to reflect the impact of the heart energy that has now surfaced. That which exists on the surface has begun to connect to and integrate with the heart and soul of the planet, which, in turn, is fully aligned with the heart and soul force of the universe. As each person opens the window through the framework of the co-creative garden to the heart and soul energy of the planet, Earth will experience what a human experiences when he consciously shifts his perceptions and suddenly releases the heart energy he holds deep within—balance and peace.

It is not enough to move about the planet in a state of benevolent love for it. Human state alone will not create the passageways through which the heart energy of the planet is allowed to release. It must be accomplished through the state of the human mind, his consciousness, combined with parallel and appropriate action. Once released, this heart energy from the planet will permeate all living reality upon its surface and support the evolutionary process of the planet and its inhabitants in tandem movement with the universe into the Aquarian era.

I fully understand that I am aligning deep planetary change and universal movement with the actions of one gardener tending one small garden. This is precisely what I mean to do. One need not wait for group

FINAL THOUGHTS

consensus in such matters. One need only move forward, sound the note for change, and follow that intonation with parallel action. Each gardener, in the role of the Knower, shall hold the seed to his heart and shall plant this seed in the earth. The fruit of this plant shall be the winged and shafted Sun above his head, and a new kingdom shall be grounded on Earth. This I can promise you. This is what awaits you.

Appendices

Kinesiology

For those of you who have never heard of kinesiology and need to learn it for the energy processes, I am reprinting information on developing kinesiology testing from the book, *Flower Essences*.

I have added some side comments to this reprinted section that might be particularly useful to Workbook II users.

KINESIOLOGY:
THE TOOL FOR TESTING

Kinesiology is simple. Everybody can do it because it links you to your electrical system and your muscles. If you are alive, you have these two things. I know that sounds smart-mouthed of me, but I've learned that sometimes people refuse to believe anything can be so simple. So they create a mental block—only "sensitive types" can do this, or only women can do this. It's just not true. Kinesiology happens to be one of those simple things in life that's waiting around to be learned and used by everyone.

If you have ever been to a chiropractor or wholistic physician, chances are you've experienced kinesiology. The doctor tells you to stick out your arm and resist his pressure. It feels like he's trying to push your arm down after he's told you not to let him do it. Everything is going fine, and then all of a sudden he presses and your arm falls down like a floppy fish. That's kinesiology.

I spell "wholistic" this way deliberately. I prefer to use a word that connotes the whole of something rather than "holistic" which, in this day and age, implies religion or holy.

KINESIOLOGY   Let me explain: If negative energy (that is, any physical object or energy that does not maintain or enhance health and balance) is introduced into a person's overall energy field, either within his body or in his immediate environment, his muscles, when having physical pressure applied, are unable to hold their strength. In other words, if pressure is applied to an individual's extended arm while his field is affected by negative energy, the arm will not be able to resist the pressure. It will weaken and fall to his side. In the case of the physician or chiropractor, they are testing specific areas of the body. When making contact with a weakened area, the muscles respond by losing their strength. If pressure is applied while connecting with a positive or balanced area, the person will easily be able to resist and the arm will hold its position.

To expand further, when negative energy is placed within a person's field, his electrical system (that electrical grid that is contained within and around his body) will immediately respond by "short-circuiting." This makes it difficult for the muscles to maintain their strength and hold the position when pressure is added. When positive energy is within the field, the electrical system holds and the muscles maintain their strength when pressure is applied.

This electrical/muscular relationship is a natural part of the human system. It is not mystical or magical. Kinesiology is the established method for reading their balance at any given moment.

If you have ever experienced muscle testing, you most likely participated in the above-described, two-man operation. You provided the extended arm and the other person provided the pressure. Although efficient, this can sometimes be cumbersome when you want to test something on your own. Arm pumpers have the nasty habit of disappearing right when you need them most. So you'll be learning to self-test—no arm pumpers needed.

NOTE FOR WORKBOOK II: Nature will communicate with you through kinesiology by projecting a positive answer (your circuit fingers will remain strong) into your system or a negative answer (your circuit fingers will weaken) into your system. By keeping the questions you ask in a simple yes/no format, you'll be able to easily communicate with nature using this system.

1. THE CIRCUIT FINGERS: **If you are right-handed:** Place your left hand palm up. Connect the tip of your left thumb with the tip of the left little finger (*not your index finger*). **If you are left-handed:** Place your right hand palm up. Connect the tip of your right thumb with the tip of your right little finger. By connecting your thumb and little finger, you have just closed an electrical circuit in your hand, and it is this circuit you will use for testing.

Before going on, look at the position you have just formed with your hand. If your thumb is touching the tip of your index or first finger, laugh at yourself for not being able to follow directions and change the position to touch the tip of the thumb with the tip of the little or fourth finger. Most likely this will not feel at all comfortable to you. If you are feeling a weird sense of awkwardness, you've got the first step of the test position! In time, the hand and fingers will adjust to being put in this position and it will feel fine.

CIRCUIT FINGERS

2. THE TEST FINGERS: To test the circuit (the means by which you will apply pressure to yourself), place the thumb and index finger of your other hand inside the circle you have created by connecting your thumb and little finger. The thumb/index finger should be right under the thumb/little finger, touching them. Don't try to make a circle with your test fingers. They're just placed inside the circuit fingers which do form a circle. It will look as if the circuit fingers are resting on the test fingers.

TEST FINGERS

3. POSITIVE RESPONSE: Keeping this position, ask yourself a yes/no question in which you already know the answer to be yes. ("Is my name _____?") Once you've asked the question, press your circuit fingers together, keeping the tip-to-tip position. *Using the same amount of pressure,* try to pull apart the circuit fingers with your test fingers. Press the lower thumb against the upper thumb, the lower index finger against the upper little finger.

Another way to say all this is that the circuit position described in step 1 corresponds to the position you take when you stick your arm out for the physician. The testing position in step 2 is in place

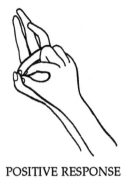

POSITIVE RESPONSE

NEGATIVE RESPONSE

of the physician or other convenient arm pumper. After you ask the yes/no question and you press your circuit fingers tip-to-tip, that's equal to the doctor saying, "Resist my pressure." Your circuit fingers now correspond to your outstretched, stiffened arm. Trying to pull apart those fingers with your testing fingers is equal to the doctor pressing down on your arm.

If the answer to the question is positive (if your name is what you think it is!), you will not be able to easily pull apart the circuit fingers. The electrical circuit will hold, your muscles will maintain their strength, and your circuit fingers will not separate. You will feel the strength in that circuit. *Important: Be sure the amount of pressure holding the circuit fingers together is equal to the amount your testing fingers press against them. Also, don't use a pumping action in your testing fingers when trying to pry your circuit fingers apart. Use an equal, steady and continuous pressure.*

Play with this a bit. Ask a few more yes/no questions that have positive answers. Now, I know it's going to seem that if you already know the answer to be yes, you are probably "throwing" the test. That's reasonable, but for the time being, until you get a feeling for what the positive response feels like in your fingers, you're going to need to deliberately ask yourself questions with positive answers.

While asking questions, if you are having trouble sensing the strength of the circuit, apply a little more pressure. Or consider that you may be applying too much pressure and pull back some. You don't have to break or strain your fingers for this; just use enough pressure to make them feel alive, connected and alert.

4. NEGATIVE RESPONSE: Once you have a clear sense of the positive response, ask yourself a question that has a negative answer. Again press your circuit fingers together and, *using equal pressure,* press against the circuit fingers with the test fingers. This time the electrical circuit will break and the circuit fingers will weaken and separate. Because the electrical circuit is broken, the muscles in the circuit fingers don't have the power to hold the fingers together. In a positive state, the electrical circuit holds and the muscles have the power to keep the two fingers together.

Play with negative questions a bit, and then return to positive questions. Get a good feeling for the strength between your circuit fingers when the electricity is in a positive state and the weakness when the electricity is in a negative state. You can even ask yourself (your own system) for a positive response and then, after testing, ask for a negative response. ("Give me a positive response." Test. "Give me a negative response." Test.) You will feel the positive strength and the negative weakness. In the beginning, you may feel only a slight difference between the two. With practice, that difference will become more pronounced. For now, it's just a matter of trusting what you've learned—and practice.

Don't forget the overall concept behind kinesiology. What enhances our body, mind and soul makes us strong. Together, our body, mind and soul create a wholistic environment which, when balanced, is strong and solid. If something enters that environment and negates or challenges the balance, the entire environment is weakened. That strength or weakness registers in the electrical system, and it can be discerned through the muscle testing technique—kinesiology.

KINESIOLOGY TIPS

If you are having trouble feeling the electrical circuit on the circuit fingers, try switching hands—the circuit fingers become the testing fingers and vice versa. Most people who are right-handed have this particular electrical circuitry in their left hand. Left-handers generally have the circuitry in their right hand. But sometimes a right-hander has the circuitry in the right hand and a left-hander has it in the left hand. You may be one of those people.

If you have an injury such as a muscle sprain in either hand or arm, don't try to learn kinesiology until you have healed. Kinesiology is muscle testing, and a muscle injury will interfere with the testing—and the testing will interfere with the healing of the muscle injury.

Also, when first learning kinesiology, do yourself a favor and set aside some quiet time to go through the instructions and play with the testing. Trying to learn this while riding the New York subway

If your testing has been going along just fine and you suddenly begin to get contradictory or "mushy" test results, consider:
1) This may not be a good day for you to do this particular work in the garden and nature is trying to alert you to this with unclear test results.
2) You need to do something else in preparation for this process and, again, nature is trying to get your attention. Ask if something else is needed first.
3) You are not in the best shape for holding a session with nature. Close everything down and come back the next day to begin the testing again.

during evening rush hour isn't going to give you the break you need. But once you have learned it, you'll be able to test all kinds of things while riding the subway.

Sometimes I meet people who are trying to learn kinesiology and aren't having much luck. They've gotten frustrated, decided this isn't for them and have gone on to try to learn another means of testing. Well, I'll listen to them explain what they did, and before they know it, I've verbally tricked them with a couple of suggestions about their testing, which they try, and they begin feeling kinesiology for the first time—a strong 'yes' and a clear 'no.' The problem wasn't kinesiology. Everyone, as I have said, has an electrical system. The problem was that they wanted to learn it so much that they became overly anxious and tense—they blocked.

So, since you won't have me around to trick you, I suggest that if you suspect you're blocking, go on to something else. Then trick yourself. When you care the least about whether or not you learn kinesiology, start playing with it again. Approach it as if it were a game. *Then* you'll feel the strength and weakness in the fingers.

Now, suppose the testing has been working fine, and then suddenly you can't get a clear result (what I call a "definite maybe") or get no result at all. Check:

1. Sloppy testing. You try to press apart the fingers before applying pressure between the circuit fingers. This happens especially when we've been testing for awhile and become over-confident or do the testing very quickly. I think it happens to all of us from time to time and serves to remind us to keep our attention on the matter at hand. (Excuse the lousy pun.)

2. External distractions. Trying to test in a noisy or active area can cause you to lose concentration. The testing will feel unsure or contradict itself if you double-check the results. Often, simply moving to a quiet, calm spot and concentrating on what you are doing will

be just what's needed for successful testing. As your testing improves, you will be able to concentrate better despite noise.

3. Focus/concentration. Even in a quiet spot, one's mind may wander and the testing will feel fuzzy, weak or contradictory. It's important to concentrate throughout the process. Check how you are feeling. If you're tired, I suggest you not try to test until you've rested a bit. And if you have to go to the bathroom, do it. That little situation is a sure concentration-destroyer.

4. The question isn't clear. A key to kinesiology is asking a *simple* yes/no question, not two questions in one, each having a possible yes/no answer. When testing for flower essences, make sure you ask one question at a time.

5. You must want to accept the results of the test. If you enter a kinesiology test not wanting to "hear" the answer, for whatever reason, you can override the test with your emotions and your will. This is true for conventional situations as well. If you really don't want something to work for you, it won't work. That's our personal power dictating the outcome.

Also, if you are trying to do testing during a situation that is especially emotional for you, that deeply stirs your emotions, or if you are trying to ask a question in which you have a strong, personal investment in the answer—such as, "Should I buy this beautiful $250,000 house?"—I suggest that you not test until you are calmer or get some emotional distance from the situation. During such times, you're walking a very fine line between a clear test and a test that your desires are overriding. Kinesiology as a tool isn't the issue here. It's the condition or intent of the tester. In fact, some questions just shouldn't be asked, but *which questions* are relative to who's doing the asking. We each need to develop discernment around which questions are appropriate for us to ask.

If you are in an emergency situation, for example, and have no choice but to test someone close who might need flower essences, be aware of your emotional vulnerability. When I am involved with testing during emotionally stressful times, I stop for a moment, collect my thoughts and make a commitment to concentrate on the testing only. If I need to test an emotionally charged question or a question about something I have a personal investment in, I stop a moment, commit myself to the test and open myself to receiving *the* answer and not the answer I might desire.

A NOTE ON CLARITY

If you're having difficulty wording a simple yes/no question, consider this an important issue to be faced and something worth spending time to rectify. You have not simply stumbled upon a glitch in your quest to use kinesiology. You've also stumbled upon a glitch in the communication between your higher self and your conscious self. If you can't even clearly phrase the question, you can't expect an answer. I've met people who cannot articulate a question. In a workshop they will attempt to ask me something and I can't figure out what they are asking—nor can anyone else in the workshop. Usually it turns out that they are frustrated because they can't get any clarity in their own life and are trying to ask me what to do about it.

For those of you who find yourselves in this boat, you have a terrific opportunity to turn that around and develop internal order by learning how to articulate a simple yes/no question. If you do this, you not only develop the tool of kinesiology, you also develop clarity for communicating with yourself. I fully understand that it will take focus on your part, and in comparison to someone who finds articulating a simple question easy, to you it will seem herculean. But if you wish to function consciously on your many levels, you must have internal clarity and order.

I recommend that you initially devote your attention to learning to ask simple questions and not worry about receiving answers. When you need to ask someone a question, take time to consider what you really want to ask and how it can be most clearly and efficiently worded. It helps to write down the question. In this way, you can visually see your words. If they don't convey what you mentally want to express, play with the wording. Keep doing this until you feel those words accurately and concisely communicate

HINT: As you develop internal order, your intuition will become clearer and stronger. You'll see that when you ask a simple yes/no question, you will intuitively sense the answer before testing. This is a normal development. I recommend that you continue with the kinesiology testing as a verification that your intuitive answer is correct.

what you wish to ask. Then go to that person and ask the question. Notice the difference in quality of how the person answers you. Your clarity will inspire similar clarity in the response.

I urge you to continue this process for a fair period of time—even dedicating yourself to the process for awhile. Quite often, that frustrating inner confusion exists because we've not had an acceptable framework for the development of mental ordering. Learning to ask questions gives the mind something tangible to work with and, in the process, you learn mind-word-and-mouth coordination. You'll find that as you develop the ability to clearly articulate a question, your inner fog will begin to lift, which in turn will automatically begin to lift your outer fog.

FINAL COMMENTS ON KINESIOLOGY

Kinesiology is like any tool. The more you practice, the better you are at using it. You need a sense of confidence about using this tool, especially when you get some very strange answers to what you thought were pretty straight questions. It helps you get over the initial "this-is-weird-and-the-damned-testing-isn't-working" stage if you have some confidence in your ability to feel clear positive and negative responses. The only way I know over this hump is to practice testing. You will develop clarity in your testing and you'll learn your personal pitfalls.

In teaching kinesiology, I have found that something interesting happens to some people when they are learning it. Every block, doubt, question and personal challenge they have, when faced head-on with something perceived as unconventional, comes right to the surface. It's as if the physical tool of kinesiology itself serves to bring to the surface all those hurdles. So they learn kinesiology right away and are using it well. Then, all of a sudden it's not working for them. When they tell me about it, I realize that the thing they do differently now that they didn't do at first is double-checking their answers—and rechecking, and rechecking, and doing it again, and again . . . Each time the answers vary or the fingers get mushy and they get "definite maybe's."

KINESIOLOGY

For those of you who already know how to use a pendulum and don't wish to learn a new tool: You may use your pendulum to distinguish the yes/no answers from nature. Just be sure to set up the processes exactly as written and ask simple yes/no questions.

Well, again the issue isn't the kinesiology. The issue is really why they are suddenly doing all this rechecking business. What have surfaced for them are questions around trust in their own ability, belief that such unconventional things really do happen and are happening to them, and a sudden lack of self-confidence.

The only way I know to get over this hurdle is to defy it—keep testing. The other alternative is to succumb and stop developing with kinesiology. But, that doesn't really accomplish anything. So in cases like this, I suggest the person keep testing, *stop* double-checking and take the plunge to go with his first test result. Eventually, what is done based on the first test result will verify the accuracy of the test. From this, your confidence builds. I firmly believe that only clear personal evidence can get us through these kinds of hurdles and blocks—and that means just continuing to go on.

So, what can we practice test on? Everything. You could easily drive yourself nuts. What colors you should wear. What colors you should wear for a special event. What would be healthiest for you to eat for breakfast, lunch and dinner. You take ten separate vitamin and mineral supplements as a matter of course on a daily basis. Try testing them individually. ("Do I need vitamin E? B$_6$? Iron?") to see if you need all ten every day. Or if there are some you don't need to take at all. You are sitting at a restaurant and they don't have Tofu Supreme on the menu. Is there anything at all on that menu that is healthy for you to eat? ("Should I eat fish?" [yes/no] "Should I eat beef?" [yes/no] "Chicken?" [yes/no] "Häagen-Dazs fudge ripple ice cream?!") And one thing you can frequently test yourself for is whether or not you need flower essences.

The point is to test everything you possibly can that doesn't place you in a life-threatening situation, follow through on your answers and then look at the results. As I have worked through the years to refine my ability to use kinesiology, I have, on many occasions, purposely followed through on answers that made no sense at all to me, just to see if the testing was accurate. Doing this and looking at the results with a critical eye is the only way I know to learn about ourselves as kinesiology testers and to discover the nuances and uses of kinesiology itself.

One last piece of information: Give yourself about a year to develop confidence with kinesiology. Now, you'll be able to use it right away. This just takes sticking with your initial efforts until you get those first feelings of positive strength and negative weakness in the circuit fingers. But I have found from my own experience and from watching others that it takes about a year of experimentation to fully learn the art of asking accurate yes/no questions, and to overcome the hurdles. As one woman said, "You stick with this stuff a year, and boy, what a great thing you end up with!"

B

Soil Balancing Kit

In order to do the Soil Balancing and Stabilizing Process and the balancing and stabilizing steps in the other energy processes, you will need to make available to the nature spirits small amounts of nutrients which, together as a set, create a balanced nutritional unit. For convenience, I made a soil balancing kit consisting of eight boxed, half-ounce bottles of the following:

Bone Meal	Cottonseed Meal
Rock Phosphate	Dolomite Lime
Nitro-10 (nitrogen)	Kelp
Greensand	Comfrey Flower Essence

Except for the Comfrey Flower Essence, these are the nutrients I add to my garden. They represent a full nutritional range and allow me to respond when doing the Soil Balancing and Stabilizing Process, no matter what is needed. If you use different organic fertilizers, that's perfectly fine—as long as you make available to nature something for phosphorus, nitrogen, potassium and the acid/alkaline balance.

If you are planning to do the process at sites away from your garden, you may wish to make a small kit also. Stopper bottles (with the glass stopper removed) or zip-lock plastic bags are convenient. You only need to have the equivalent of about three tablespoons of each nutrient—and that can last you for 20 processes.

For those of you who use animal manures only: the above additives are preferred over animal manures because of the depth of the work. One normally does not find cow manure five feet below the surface of the ground. But greensand, rock phosphate and bone meal can be integrated into that molecular level without changing the character of the soil.

I have expanded my kit to include the extra nutrients and trace minerals. They are:

Alfalfa	Manganese
Boron	Potassium
Calcium	Salt
Chromium	Zinc
Copper	Molybdenum
Iron	Sulfur
Magnesium	Liquid Seaweed

I have gotten the mineral balancers in the form of regular mineral supplements that are found in drug stores and health food stores. The balancers included in the basic kit are ordered from:

Mellinger's Inc.
2310 W. South Range Rd.
North Lima, OH 44452-9731
Tel: 800/321-7444

They'll be glad to send you their catalog upon request.

However, for those of you who:

1. live in the city and have no access to organic fertilizers, don't wish to store 50-lb. bags of bone meal and rock phosphate in your pantry, but wish to work with the Soil Balancing and Stabilizing Process in your environment,

2. live anywhere but have no garden and don't plan to have one and also don't have easy access to the fertilizers, but wish to work with the processes,

3. have a garden or farm and are firm believers of using animal

manures only, but would like to incorporate the energy processes that require the other organic fertilizers and don't wish to purchase bags of it just to make a little kit,

I am offering the Soil Balancing Process kit. Ordering information is in the back of this book. A single half-ounce bottle will give you about 20 tests.

FLOWER ESSENCES

If you would like to know more about flower essences, I am reprinting the section on flower essences from our catalog. As part of the co-creative garden work here at Perelandra, we produce three sets of flower essences: Perelandra Rose Essences, Perelandra Garden Essences and Perelandra Rose Essences II. I offer you the our information in the spirit of giving you general information about flower essences and specific information about our essences. I don't like to leave folks with the impression that the Perelandra essences are the only flower essences in the world, so at the end of appendix C is a list of other flower essences producers who will be happy to send you their catalogs on request.

In using flower essences as stabilizers during the Soil Balancing and Stabilizing Process, I suggest that the Rose, Garden and Rose II sets be added to your kit.

You folks have the opportunity to use flower essences in two ways:

1. As stabilizers for the Soil Balancing and Stabilizing Process that you will be doing as part of most of the energy processes discussed in this book.

2. As part of a personal health and balancing program. The following will give you a clearer idea of how the essences work with us.

FROM THE PERELANDRA CATALOG:

The human body has within and surrounding it an electrical network. When we experience health, this electrical network is balanced and fully connected. When something in our life or environment threatens that balance, the electrical system responds by either short-circuiting or overloading. That imbalance in the electrical system immediately impacts the central nervous system. The body then goes into high gear in an effort to correct the imbalance. If our body does not succeed, we physically manifest the imbalance. We get a cold or a headache or our allergy pops up again or another migraine belts us. Or we get back pain or our neck goes out again. Or we become seriously ill.

This is the same electrical system that we work with when doing kinesiology testing.

Flower essences work directly with both the electrical and the central nervous systems. By taking the correct essences, we immediately balance the electrical system, stabilize the nervous system and stop the domino effect that leads to illness.

If we don't take the essences and wind up getting sick, we can still take the essence(s) which will then stabilize and balance the electrical and nervous systems while the body gets on with the business of fighting off the problem. By assisting this process, flower essences drastically reduce our recovery time. In short, by using the essences, we are not asking our body to pull double duty—work to heal us systemically *and* rebalance our electrical and central nervous systems.

A different perspective about the essences, excerpted from a session given by the Deva of Flower Essences in the book, *Flower Essences*, might be helpful:

> . . . *You are getting the idea that all is changing. How one perceives his health is also changing. As with everything around him, the key to this change is balance. One's health will be intimately linked with one's understanding and response to balance.*
>
> . . . *They [flower essences] support and help secure balance on all levels—physical, emotional, mental and spiritual. Physically, they balance the body by reconnecting and adjusting the*

electrical system. Emotionally and mentally, they help the person identify, alter and sometimes remove emotional and mental patterns that challenge his overall balance. And spiritually, they assist the person's connection to and understanding of the many levels of himself so that he can operate in life from a broader perspective.

Flower essences provide a health system that is aligned to both the surrounding universal dynamics of transition, and the individual's expansion and response to the times by having incorporated within the system itself the key to it all—balance.

The Perelandra flower essences have been a natural development in the work that has gone on between nature and myself. They are produced from the flowers, vegetables and herbs grown in the Perelandra garden. The essences are carefully prepared and stabilized pattern-infused water tinctures that are then preserved in brandy. The tinctures go through a final stabilization inside the genesa crystal sitting in the center of the garden. They are bottled in a *concentrate form* in pharmaceutical dropper bottles that make it easy and convenient for you to place one drop of a needed essence directly on your tongue or several drops of the essence in a glass of water to be sipped throughout the day.

I feel that through these flower essences we are able to share the extraordinary vitality and power that has resulted from the co-creative work with nature in the Perelandra garden. In using the essences, we establish another partnership with nature—this one focused on our health, balance and well-being.

If you are intrigued, interested or curious about flower essences and wish to investigate them further, I offer some suggestions on how you might proceed without feeling overwhelmed.

❋ Read *Flower Essences: Reordering Our Understanding and Approach to Illness and Health.* It will give you a crystal-clear idea about what flower essences are, the testing techniques and processes used, how to choose the essences you need and suggestions on how to successfully integrate them into your life. The Perelandra essences are fully discussed, but the book is applicable to all flower essences and

FLOWER ESSENCES   presents step-by-step processes that can be used for any essences on the market. (If you already have a set of essences and wish to use them with greater effectiveness and precision, you still might consider getting the book, *Flower Essences*.)

✿ For those who would like to try essences and experience how they work: Read through the Perelandra essence definitions that are listed in this appendix. Then think about some physical, emotional, mental or spiritual problem you would like to address. Think of it clearly or even write it out. Then say to yourself, "What essence(s) do I need to help me with this problem now?" Read through the definitions again and note which one(s) intuitively pop out to you. (If you know kinesiology, you can simply test the list of essences, choosing the ones which test positive for you.) Order the essences that stand out when you read the definitions. (Try to keep your rational mind out of the process!) You'll get a Guide with the bottles which will explain how to use them and teach you how to find out how often to take them. Usually one drop, once or twice daily for several days will do the trick. Then see how you feel. Also, get the book *Flower Essences* so that you can see more clearly when and how they are to be used.

✿ For those, like myself, who are immediately struck between the eyes by these things called "flower essences" and know they belong in your life: I strongly suggest that you get the **Basic Set** of Perelandra essences. That is, **the Rose Essences (set I) and the Garden Essences.** This is an excellent starter combination for day-to-day process and issues. Now, to be honest with you, I've been reluctant to suggest this to people. I'm sensitive to the fact that we're talking about money here and, as the producer/developer of the Perelandra essences, there is an obvious conflict of interest in my suggestion. But I feel urged to come out of the closet with this suggestion for three reasons:

1. These two sets often work in *combination* with one another. The Rose Essences address and support the various steps of the transition process we move through as we face daily challenge and change. The Garden Essences address specific issues on the physical, emotional, mental and spiritual levels (PEMS) that either trigger

transition or arise because of it. In my work as an essence practitioner, I have found that often a person needs support for both the transition process itself and the specific issues coming up due to the process.

2. The Basic Set of Perelandra essences covers a full range of transition issues and specific issues. What is needed this week will often be different from what is needed next week or next month or next year. The essences are used one or two drops at a time and have an indefinite shelf life. In short, you'll be keeping and using the set for many years. It's fair to assume that you or someone close to you will be needing each of the essences at some point. It's more convenient to have them on hand when needed rather than have to order those specific bottles and wait for them to arrive in the mail before using them.

3. I've noticed over the past years that a fair number of people initially ordering single bottles or partial sets end up ordering the Basic Set. After using them, they came to the conclusion that to use the essences with the greatest of agility and accuracy, one needs to have on hand the full range provided by the Basic Set of Perelandra essences.

I also suggest that when ordering the Basic Set of Perelandra essences, you include *Flower Essences* along with your order. I know I am suggesting this book a lot. But I feel strongly that it will help you to organize and integrate the essences into your life in a precise and extremely effective manner.

In 1992, we added a new set of flower essences: Perelandra Rose Essences II. This set of eight essences addresses the body's eight specific functions that are activated and/or impacted during a deep expansion experience. These experiences, by nature, require that we address and integrate something completely new and, as a result, we change our personal and world view. Here, one is not processing ordinary, everyday occurrences. Rather, one is faced with an experience that challenges the body's capability to balance and function. It seems like many people are experiencing deep expansion. If you are interested in incorporating flower essences in your life, I suggest that you also include this new set along with the Basic Set of Perelandra Rose and Garden Essences.

With each purchase, individual bottles or sets, you get the beginner's Guide which gives the step-by-step basic processes for accurately testing yourself for the essences you need and discerning the correct dosage—i.e., how many drops of the essences are needed for how many days. Also included in the Guide are the long definitions for each of the essences. Reading them will give you a clearer idea of what the essences address.

THE PERELANDRA ROSE ESSENCES

The Perelandra Rose Essences are a set of eight flower essences. Made from roses in the Perelandra garden, these eight essences function with one another to support and balance an individual's physical body and soul as he proceeds forward in *day-to-day evolutionary process*. As we move forward in daily process, there are mechanisms within us which are set in motion to facilitate our periods of growth. The Perelandra Rose Essences help to stabilize and balance us and our process mechanisms.

The following are short definitions of the Perelandra Rose Essences. The name of each essence is the same as the rose from which it is made.

GRUSS AN AACHEN: Stability. Balances and stabilizes the body/soul unit on all PEMS levels (physical, emotional, mental, spiritual) as it moves forward in its evolutionary process.

PEACE: Courage. Opens the individual to the inner dynamic of courage that is aligned to universal courage.

ECLIPSE: Acceptance and insight. Enhances the individual's appreciation of his own inner knowing. Supports the mechanism which allows the body to receive the soul's input and insight.

ORANGE RUFFLES: Receptivity. Stabilizes the individual during the expansion of his sensory system.

AMBASSADOR: Pattern. Aids the individual in seeing the relationship of the part to the whole, in perceiving his pattern and purpose.

NYMPHENBURG: Strength. Supports and holds the strength created by the balance of the body/soul fusion, and facilitates the individual's ability to regain that balance.

WHITE LIGHTNIN': Synchronized movement. Stabilizes the inner timing of all PEMS levels moving in concert, and enhances the body/soul fusion.

ROYAL HIGHNESS: Final stabilization. The mop-up essence which helps to insulate, protect and stabilize the individual and to stabilize the shift during its final stages while vulnerable.

THE PERELANDRA GARDEN ESSENCES

This set of eighteen essences is made from the flower petals of vegetables, herbs and flowers grown in the Perelandra garden. Their balancing and restorative patterns address physical, emotional, mental and spiritual *issues* that we face in today's world.

BROCCOLI: For the power balance which must be maintained when one perceives himself to be under seige from outside. Stabilizes the body/soul unit so the person won't close down, detach and scatter.

CAULIFLOWER: Stabilizes and balances the child during the birth process.

CELERY: Restores balance of the immune system during times when it is being overworked or stressed, and during long-term viral or bacterial infections.

CHIVES: Re-establishes the power one has when the internal male/female dynamics are balanced and the person is functioning in a state of awareness within this balance.

COMFREY: Repairs higher vibrational soul damage that occurred in the present or a past lifetime.

CORN: Stabilization during universal/spiritual expansion. Assists transition of experience into useful, pertinent understanding and action.

CUCUMBER: Rebalancing during depression. Vital reattachment to life.

DILL: Assists individual in reclaiming power balance one has released to others. Victimization.

NASTURTIUM: Restores vital physical life energy during times of intense mental-level focus.

OKRA: Returns ability to see the positive in one's life and environment.

SALVIA: Restores emotional stability during times of extreme stress.

SNAP PEA: Rebalances child or adult after a nightmare. Assists in ability to translate daily experience into positive, understandable process.

SUMMER SQUASH: Restores courage to the person who experiences fear and resistance when faced with daily routine. Shyness. Phobia.

SWEET BELL PEPPER: Inner peace, clarity and calm when faced with today's stressful times. Stabilizes body/soul balance during times of stress.

TOMATO: Cleansing. Assists the body in shattering and throwing off that which is causing infection or disease.

YELLOW YARROW: Emotional protection during vulnerable times. Its support softens resistance and assists the integration process.

ZINNIA: Reconnects one to the child within. Restores playfulness, laughter, joy and a sense of healthy priorities.

ZUCCHINI: Helps restore physical strength during convalescence.

PERELANDRA ROSE ESSENCES II

This is the new set of Perelandra flower essences. The eight essences are made from roses in the garden and address the eight specific functions within the body that are activated and/or impacted during a *deep expansion experience*. Here, one is not simply processing ordinary, everyday occurrences. Rather, one is faced with an experience that is new and challenging to the present balance and functioning of the body. When faced with this kind of expansion, the body is required to function in ways that are new and with patterns and rhythms yet to be experienced. The new Rose Essences II address this expansion phenomenon by fine-tuning, balancing and stabilizing the specific steps of the process one must go through to expand.

It is an individual's soul that chooses to make deep changes. However, the individual's body does not have the patterning within its process mechanisms to deal with these more profound changes. The development and utilization of new ways of functioning to meet new needs which cannot be effectively processed by existing means is what defines an expansion experience and distinguishes it from an everyday life process.

I wish I could list specific experiences that would identify deep expansion situations for you, but a deep expansion for some is an everyday life process for others. The only thing I can say is that if you are interested in Perelandra and incorporating flower essences in your life, you are the kind of person who doesn't shy away from deep expansion. I think it would be good to have a set of Rose Essences II handy.

The following are the short definitions for the Rose Essences II. The name of each essence is the same as the name of the rose from which it is made.

BLAZE IMPROVED CLIMBING ROSE: Softens and relaxes first the central nervous system and then the body as a whole, thus allowing the input from an expansion experience to be appropriately sorted, shifted and integrated within the body.

MAYBELLE STEARNS: Stabilizes and supports the sacrum during an expansion experience.

MR. LINCOLN: Balances and stabilizes the cerebrospinal fluid (CSF) pulse while it alters its rhythm and patterning to accommodate the expansion.

SONIA: Stabilizes and supports the CSF pulse *after* it has completed its shift to accommodate the expansion.

CHICAGO PEACE: Stabilizes movement of and interaction among the cranial bones, CSF and sacrum during an expansion experience.

BETTY PRIOR: Stabilizes and balances the delicate rhythm of expansion and contraction of the cranial bones during the expansion.

TIFFANY: Stabilizes the cranials as they shift their alignment appropriately to accommodate the input and impulses of expansion.

OREGOLD: Stabilizes and balances the cranials, central nervous system, CSF and sacrum after an expansion process is complete.

PERELANDRA ESSENCES
PURCHASING INFORMATION

BASIC SET: Perelandra Rose & Garden Essences. Both full sets purchased together. Available in 1-dram (1/8 oz.) and half-ounce bottles. Perhaps it might help you to decide which size set is best for you if I point out a couple of things.

1) Obviously, the half-ounce set is more economical. It is 4 times larger than the dram set. It consists of the 26 Perelandra Rose & Garden Essences in a total of 3 boxes.

2) The dram set contains the 26 Perelandra Rose & Garden Essences in one box that measures approximately 6-by-8-inches. This is convenient if you are planning to take the essences on trips or shift them between home and office.

BASIC SET WITH BOOK: The 26 Perelandra Rose & Garden Essences plus the book, *Flower Essences: Reordering Our Understanding and Approach to Illness and Health.* Essences are available in 1-dram and half-ounce bottles.

EXPANDED SET: Includes the Basic Set (Perelandra Rose & Garden Essences) plus the new Perelandra Rose Essences II set.

EXPANDED SET WITH BOOK: The Basic Rose & Garden Essences plus the new Perelandra Rose Essences II and the book, *Flower Essences*.

PERELANDRA ROSE ESSENCES SET: Includes eight boxed, dropper bottles (1/2-oz, only), the Guide and the short-definitions card for quick reference.

PERELANDRA ROSE ESSENCES II SET: Includes eight boxed, dropper bottles (1/2-oz. only), the Guide and the short-definitions card for quick referrence.

PERELANDRA GARDEN ESSENCES SET: Two boxes containing a total of eighteen dropper bottles (1/2-oz. only), the Guide and two short-definitions cards.

INDIVIDUAL ESSENCES: Half-ounce dropper bottles, plus the Guide. NOTE: We offer only 1/2-oz. bottles for refilling empty bottles in the dram set. One bottle will give you 4 dram refills.

NEWEST ESSENCE DEVELOPMENTS: The Perelandra Nature Program Essences, developed in 1993, include a boxed set of nine 1/2-oz. dropper bottles, a Guide and a short-definitions card. In 1994, the Perelandra Soul Ray Essences were developed. They include a boxed set of eight 1/2-oz. dropper bottles, a Guide, and the short-definitions card. For a full description of these two extraordinary essence sets, please see the Perelandra catalog.

For prices and ordering information, see the order form at the end of this book.

If you would like information about the workshops and open house or would like to be on our mailing list, just send us a note. We'll be glad to send you our catalog, as well.

OTHER FLOWER ESSENCES SOURCES

Flower Essence Services
P.O. Box 1769
Nevada City, CA 95959

Australian Bush Essences
Box 531
Spit Junction, NSW
Australia 2088

Alaskan Flower Essence Project
P.O. Box 1369
Fritz Creek, AK 99603

The Dr. Edward Bach Healing
Society: U.S./Canada Distributor
P.O. Box 320
Woodmere, NY 11598

A Bit about Perelandra and My Research with Nature

Perelandra is both home for Clarence and me and a nature research center. It now consists of forty-five acres of mostly woods in the foothills of the Blue Ridge Mountains in Virginia. The nature research and development has been going on since 1976, when I dedicated myself to learning about nature in new ways from nature itself. I began working with nature intelligences in a coordinated, co-creative and educational effort which has resulted in understanding and demonstrating a new approach to agriculture and ecological balance. Besides publishing materials about the research, we hold an annual workshop series and open house at Perelandra. *Except for these scheduled days, Perelandra is closed to the public in order to have the time and space needed for the continuing research work.*

The primary focus of my work has been the one-hundred-foot-diameter circular garden where I get from nature the information and direction I need to create an all-inclusive garden environment based on the principles of energy in balance. For example, we do not attempt to repel insects. Instead, we focus on creating a balanced environment that calls to it and fully supports a complete and appropriate population of insects. In turn, the insects relate to the garden's plant life in a light and nondestructive manner.

From this kind of work has developed a new method of gardening which I call "co-creative gardening." Briefly, this is a method of gardening in partnership with the nature intelligences that emphasizes balance and teamwork. The balance is a result of concentrating on the laws of form and the life energy behind form. The teamwork is established between the individual and the intelligent levels inherent in nature. (Information about this work is described in three books: *Behaving As If the God In All Life Mattered*, *Perelandra Garden Workbook: A Complete Guide to Gardening with Nature Intelligences*, and *Perelandra Garden Workbook II: Co-Creative Energy Processes for Gardening, Agriculture and Life*.)

The foundation of the work going on at Perelandra, as I have indicated, comes from nature intelligences, a collective term I use for devas and nature spirits. My work with flower essences and a number of physical health and balancing processes have also been directed from these levels. Therefore, it might be helpful if I gave you *my* idea of who and what these intelligences are.

"Deva" is a sanskrit word used to describe the intelligent level of consciousness within nature that functions in an architectural mode within all that is form and also serves as the organizer of all that is a part of each form.

"Nature spirit" refers to the intelligent level of consciousness within nature that works in partnership with the devic level and is responsible for the fusing and maintaining of energy to appropriate five-senses form. Nature spirits tend to the shifting of an energy reality that has been formulated on the devic level and assist the translation of that reality from a dynamic of energy to five-senses form. They also function in a custodial capacity with all that is form on the planet.

My work with nature intelligences continues on at a pace and scope that oftentimes amazes me. I am convinced that I could work with nature for the rest of time and still not know or understand all the pieces and possibilities the reality of nature represents.

PERELANDRA GARDEN WORKBOOK II
ORDER FORM

___ *Behaving as if the God in All Life Mattered* (updated and revised) .... $12.95 *

___ *Dancing in the Shadows of the Moon* (hardcover) $23.00

___ *Perelandra Garden Workbook: A Complete Guide to Gardening with Nature Intelligences* (2nd edition) $19.95

___ *Perelandra Garden Workbook II: Co-Creative Energy Processes for Gardening, Agriculture and Life* $16.95

___ *Flower Essences: Reordering Our Understanding and Approach to Illness and Health* $10.95

___ *MAP: The Co-Creative White Brotherhood Medical Assistance Program* (2nd edition) .... $14.95 *

___ *Perelandra Microbial Balancing Program Manual* $16

* These books are also available in Spanish. See the Perelandra Catalog for details.

___ Perelandra Soil Balancing Process Kit $14.95

___ Free catalog of all Perelandra products

PERELANDRA ESSENCES

___ Basic Set: Perelandra Rose & Garden Essences (1/2 oz.) $102

___ Basic Set: Perelandra Rose & Garden Essences (Dram) $74

___ Expanded Set: Perelandra Rose, Garden & Rose II Essences (1/2-oz.) $136

___ Expanded Set: Perelandra Rose, Garden & Rose II Essences (Dram) $95

___ Basic Set (Rose & Garden Essences) with book, *Flower Essences* (1/2 oz.) $110

___ Basic Set (Rose & Garden Essences) with book, *Flower Essences* (Dram) $82

___ Expanded Set (Perelandra Rose, Garden & Rose II) with book, *Flower Essences* (1/2-oz.) $144

___ Expanded Set (Perelandra Rose, Garden & Rose II) with book, *Flower Essences* (Dram) $103

___ Perelandra Nature Program Essences Set (1/2 oz. bottles only) $47
      (When purchased with an Expanded Set of flower essences .... $42)

___ Perelandra Soul Ray Essences Set (1/2-oz. bottles only) $42
      (When purchased with an Expanded Set of flower essences .... $37)

___ Perelandra Rose Essences Set (1/2 oz. bottles only) $40

___ Perelandra Rose Essences II Set (1/2-oz. bottles only) $40

___ Perelandra Garden Essences Set (1/2 oz. bottles only) $78

___ Individual Essences (1/2 oz. bottles only) Please list below .... $6.50 each *

□ *Please preserve the essences I have ordered in vinegar instead of brandy.*

_____

_____

☞ * *Save 20% when ordering a total of **eight or more** individual flower essences of any type; each bottle then ... **$5.20***

Perelandra
P.O. Box 3603
Warrenton, VA 20188
24-Hour Phone: 800/960-8806 or 540/937-2153 (answering machines)
24-Hour Fax: 540/937-3360
http://www.perelandra-ltd.com

Send to (please print):

Name: _____

Address (UPS): _____

_____

City & State: _____ Zip: _____

Phone: _____ Fax: _____

U.S. POSTAGE & HANDLING

under $8.00 . . . . 2.20	$100.01 to 200.00 . . . . 9.40
$8.01 to 14.00 . . . . 4.00	$200.01 to 300.00 . . . . 11.50
$14.01 to 25.00 . . . . 5.00	$300.01 & over . . . . . . 5% of order
$25.01 to 50.00 . . . . 6.00	
$50.01 to 75.00 . . . . 7.30	**AK, HI, VI & PR:** Subtotal over $50, please
$75.01 to 100.00 . . . . . . 8.30	send 1 1/2 times chart. (Shipped first class.)

International shipping rates are available upon request.

Subtotal _____		
− 15% Senior Discount _____		
Sales Tax: 4.5%* _____		
Postage & Handling** _____		
Total _____		

* Sales tax is for Virginia residents only.
** Postage based on pre-discount price.

Method of Payment: ☐ Check ☐ Money Order ☐ Visa ☐ MasterCard ☐ Discover

Card Number: _____

Expiration Date: _____

Signature: _____

Credit card orders must be accompanied by signature.

NOTE: Prices and shipping charges are subject to change without notice.